MW01155963

Every Kid a Writer

Strategies That Get Everyone Writing

KELLY BOSWELL

HEINEMANN
Portsmouth, NH

Heinemann
361 Hanover Street
Portsmouth, NH 03801–3912
www.heinemann.com

Offices and agents throughout the world

© 2021 by Kelly Boswell

All rights reserved. No part of this book may be reproduced in any form or by any electronic or mechanical means, including information storage and retrieval systems, without permission in writing from the publisher, except by a reviewer, who may quote brief passages in a review, and with the exception of reproducibles (identified by the *Every Kid a Writer: Strategies That Get Everyone Writing* copyright line), which may be photocopied for classroom use.

> *Heinemann's authors have devoted their entire careers to developing the unique content in their works, and their written expression is protected by copyright law. We respectfully ask that you do not adapt, reuse, or copy anything on third-party (whether for-profit or not-for-profit) lesson-sharing websites.*
> **—Heinemann Publishers**

"Dedicated to Teachers" is a trademark of Greenwood Publishing Group, Inc.

The author and publisher wish to thank those who have generously given permission to reprint borrowed material:

Excerpts from Common Core State Standards © Copyright 2010. National Governors Association Center for Best Practices and Council of Chief State School Officers. All rights reserved.

Library of Congress Cataloging-in-Publication Data

Name: Boswell, Kelly, author.
Title: Every kid a writer : strategies that get everyone writing / by Kelly Boswell.
Description: Portsmouth, NH : Heinemann, [2020] | Includes bibliographical references.
Identifiers: LCCN 2020017942 | ISBN 9780325092294 (paperback)
Subjects: LCSH: English language—Composition and exercises—Study and teaching (Elementary) | English language—Composition and exercises—Study and teaching (Secondary)
Classification: LCC LB1576 .B5315 2020 | DDC 372.62/3—dc23
LC record available at https://lccn.loc.gov/2020017942

Editorial: Tobey Antao
Production: Kimberly Capriola
Cover and interior designs: Monica Ann Crigler
Typesetting: Gina Poirier, Gina Poirier Design
Manufacturing: Steve Bernier

Printed in the United States of America on acid-free paper
1 2 3 4 5 6 7 8 9 10   VP   25 24 23 22 21 20
October 2020 Printing

To the teachers, students, instructional coaches, and principals
at Centennial, Dorothy Moses, Liberty, Lincoln, Northridge,
Pioneer, Prairie Rose, and Sunrise Elementary Schools
in Bismarck, North Dakota.

"Day by day you have to give the work before you
all the best stuff you have, not saving up for later projects.
If you give freely, there will always be more."
—Anne Lamott, author of *Bird by Bird*

CONTENTS

FOREWORD
by Harvey "Smokey" Daniels

You are about to spend nearly 200 pages with a sparkling and generous mind. I first met Kelly Boswell in 2012, when we were hired separately to consult in a rural school district, she with the elementary teachers and I with the secondary. I'd seen some of her earlier books, and we'd said hi at conferences, but we'd never worked together. Our first task was to plan and co-teach an opening workshop for all the town's K–12 teachers. We got on the phone and cooked something up before we hopped on different planes. The next morning, I did an opening segment and then handed it over to Kelly, as planned. She stood up and proceeded to wow the assembled educators. Have you ever had this thing happen where you are listening to someone talk, and you realize that every word coming out of their mouth is just, like, the Truth? That's the feeling I get now, hearing Kelly's voice again in these pages.

So, have you ever encountered any "reluctant" writers in your classes over the years? Well, of course you have—we all have! Some days our classrooms seem to be crammed with countless kids who are staring, dawdling, avoiding, postponing, sidestepping, malingering, or otherwise *not writing* when time is offered. Kelly calls this phenomenon "the shrug, the slump, and the sharpening of pencils."

But before we start to blame the kids for this reluctance, Kelly says, let's look at ourselves. Have *we* ever behaved like this when faced with a writing task? Well, no, not when we've written a grocery list. But wait. Writing a term paper for a graduate school class? Yikes, no, how can I get out of this! The point is that *every* would-be author, child or adult, is reluctant to write some of the time. Instead of bemoaning this simple reality, we need to get on with clearing a path for the fearful. Hence this book.

This guide is much like Kelly's live presentations. Her suggestions are clear, practical, and doable—bubbling with kid smartness and teacherly humor. Kelly has a straightforward formula for reducing students' writing reluctance and enhancing their confidence and fluency:

1. Use mentors and modeling to fuel engagement.

2. Create a safe and daily space for writing.

3. Expose writers to real readers.

4. Offer choice.

5. Maintain a healthy perspective on conventions.

6. Shape writing identity through assessment.

In each chapter, she offers lessons, classroom stories, kid dialogues, plans, models, and teacher moves. Also in every chapter, Kelly shows exactly how kids can meet all state and national standards when these five conditions guide instruction.

While there is a dedicated chapter on teacher modeling, this vital and oft-neglected theme runs powerfully through the whole book. As Kelly gently coaches us, "Modeling doesn't require you to write perfectly. When you write in front of your kids, you're not modeling perfection; you're modeling process. You're showing them how you think, plan, make decisions, cross things out, change your mind, revise, and persevere. You're showing them how writers write."

In Kelly's chapter on the conventions of writing, there is a scene that especially charmed me, one of many graceful metaphors scattered through the book. Kelly is in her kitchen, trying to teach her two frisky sons how to bake.

> I found myself tensing up when watching my sons crack eggs or measure (not so precisely) that cup of flour. As an adult who has been baking for a good number of years, I've grown to be fairly precise in my measuring and recipe following. Baking with my kids required me to relax a bit on the "rules of baking" so that we could enjoy the *process*. I came to realize that it wasn't as important that they followed the recipe *exactly* or that they measured *correctly*. Give or take a little bit would be OK, as long as they would discover a love of baking or spending time in the kitchen creating something to be shared with others.
>
> Don't get me wrong. There were a few basic and non-negotiable principles that I knew I needed to teach them: Don't eat raw eggs. Wash your hands before you begin. You can't substitute

salt for sugar. There are standard units of measurement that we use when we bake. It's imperative that you add a half *teaspoon* of salt rather than a half *cup* of salt.

But if I wanted to help my boys grow into men who would know their way around a kitchen (and how to make a decent batch of chocolate chip cookies), I needed to hold these two goals in tension: teach them the basic rules of baking *and* help them enjoy the process of baking. If I focused too heavily on the rules and on baking *correctly*, my kids might learn how to bake, but it's unlikely that they would enjoy it and choose to continue baking.

Same with writing.

As someone who has been publishing with Heinemann since 1985, I am tremendously proud to welcome Kelly Boswell to our family of authors.

Now, reader, don't be reluctant. Come and cook in Kelly's kitchen!

Harvey "Smokey" Daniels
Santa Fe, New Mexico

ACKNOWLEDGMENTS

It has been a tremendous honor to work with the incredible team at Heinemann. My eternal gratitude to Vicki Boyd, Roderick Spelman, Sarah Fournier, Catrina Marshall Swasey, Patty Adams, Kimberly Capriola, Suzanne Heiser, Monica Crigler, Jillian Sims, and Kalli Kirkpatrick. And special thanks to the PD team: Mim Easton, Michelle Flynn, Cheryl Savage, and Cherie Bartlett who support me in the work I do with teachers.

My editor, Tobey Antao, was much more than an editor. She was a cheerleader, thought partner, coach, mentor, and friend. Her keen sense of reading and writing, brilliant insights, savvy observations, and sharp wit have helped to shape this book in so many ways. Tobey nudged and encouraged in all the right ways and helped *this* less-than-enthused writer finish strong. Thank you, Tobey.

I have been fortunate and incredibly blessed to know and learn from Harvey "Smokey" Daniels. Smokey is a tireless advocate for excellence, a champion for all learners, and one of the smartest and most genuine people I know. He lives a joyfully curious life and invites all of us to do the same. I am humbled and so grateful that Smokey crafted the foreword for this book. It means the world to me.

I stand on the shoulders of so many researchers, authors, and teachers who have championed best practice in writing instruction while honoring and respecting children's voices. Some of them I have never met, and some of them I cherish as dear friends. Each of them has shaped the way I teach writing and approach teaching. I owe an immeasurable debt of gratitude to Richard Allington, Carl Anderson, Lucy Calkins, Harvey "Smokey" Daniels, Peter Elbow, Ralph Fletcher, Kelly Gallagher, Matt Glover, Donald Graves, Mary Howard, Linda Hoyt, Penny Kittle, Joan Moser, Don Murray, Tom Newkirk, Regie Routman, Vicki Spandel, Tony Stead, and Katie Wood Ray.

I am fortunate to have many thought partners, coaches, colleagues, peers, and friends who help me reflect about teaching and learning and help me grow and stretch my thinking: Kerry Bishop, Vanessa Bobbit, Kristy Castor, Sarah Dunkin, Julie Frank, Heidi Freeman, Lindsay Jacobson, Jan Martin,

Renée Niepoky, Sherri Nissen, Christina Nosek, Renee Sacco, Ann Stewart, Jenna White, and Kari Yates.

A special thank-you to my mentor and friend Linda Hoyt, who encouraged me to write long before I had the courage to put any words to paper. Thank you for opening so many doors of opportunity to me.

Thank you to the talented and enormously kind Rebecca Brick, whose photographs grace the pages of this book. And to Chris Job, Jill Vallejo, Michelle Fitterer, Christy Karch, Ashley Dressler, and Katie Larson at Lincoln Elementary, thank you for opening up your school and classrooms to us.

Deep gratitude goes to the teachers who generously shared student samples with me, invited me in to watch them teach, or allowed me into their classrooms to teach and learn alongside them: Karen Arnold, Michele Beitel, Renae Ely, Julie Frank, Whitney Fridley, Macie Harris, Holly Hart, Kathy Haskins, Ariann Hess-Headlee, Anna Jaross, Rylee Meir, Lisa Miller, Sherri Nissen, Hanh-Nhi Pham, Tina Pletan, Melissa Potts, Tamara Ward, Aly Weigel, and Kristin Wild.

To my parents, Tom and Hazel Jay, and my husband's parents, Ben and Claudia Boswell—all retired teachers who continue to be lifelong thinkers, learners, and leaders—thank you for your constant support and for showing me what it looks like to live life well.

To my sisters, Ginger Jay and Tamara Ward, and my brother-in-law, David Casteal—educators, instructional leaders, and advocates for all students—I am in awe of what you do for the learners in your care each day. And special thanks to Candy and Ava Casteal. Your love and support mean the world to me.

To Carson and Brady: You keep things real and help me to create exceptionally cool playlists. Wherever you go, go with all of your heart. P.S. Kindly pick up the thousands and thousands and thousands of Legos that lie strewn about our house. Seriously.

Finally, I could not have written this book without the tenacious love and steadfast support of my best friend and husband. Corwin, you are the gravitational pull that holds everything together.

Chapter One

The Shrug, the Slump, and the Sharpening of Pencils

The teaching of writing is enormously exciting only if we expect it to be, that is, only if we expect our students to write interesting essays, only if we read and listen carefully between the lines, only if we are honest with them and with ourselves.

—Lad Tobin, author and writing professor

If you've been teaching for any length of time, you've probably lived through a scene like this:

You wrap up your well-planned and fairly well-executed writing lesson, give some final words of wisdom, and send your students off to begin writing. Out of the corner of your eye, you notice a few kids walking briskly (OK, *running*) toward the bathroom passes hanging by the door, each of them hoping to be the first one to grab a pass and scoot right on out the door.

You turn your attention toward the remaining students, who have begun to settle in. A few are scrawling with furrowed brows, deep in thought. Yet you can't help but notice that some of them are . . . well . . . *dawdling.* A handful of kids have suddenly discovered that their pencils are in need of a good, long sharpening. One student has noticed a thread that has come loose on his sweatshirt and is slowly and meticulously wrapping the thread around his index finger.

If the picture I've painted sounds even vaguely familiar to you, rest assured that you are not alone. Many of us find ourselves surrounded by a few (or perhaps more than a few) students who shrug when asked about their writing. They slump in their chairs instead of jumping into writing with energy and vigor. They sharpen pencils or ask for the bathroom pass or decide it's a good time to organize and reorganize their desk. They groan when you announce that it's time to write, or they barrage you with questions along the lines of "How long does this have to be?" They start but rarely finish pieces of writing, or they write the bare minimum and then shout a hearty, *I'm done!*

From our perspective, it might look as though these students are looking for *any* excuse *not* to write. They might appear to be what we sometimes call "reluctant writers"—kids who know how to write but are unwilling to write or seem to have an aversion to writing.

This picture I've painted—these kids who seem disinterested and disengaged—can be incredibly disheartening, especially when you've invested precious time and energy thoughtfully planning a lesson or a unit or a writing experience that you thought would be engaging and powerful.

"What can we do?" we might wonder.

First, let's start by taking a closer look at one of these writers: *you.*

Reflect on Your Own Life as a Writer

Think back to a time when writing was painful or when you didn't want to write. Maybe that thesis paper in college. Or that biography you wrote in sixth grade. Or an email to a parent that you wrote last week. Have you captured the memory in your mind? In my work, when I've asked teachers to share these memories (and when I've shared these memories from my own writing life), I've noticed some similarities in our experiences. Do these also ring true for you?

- Time seemed to *slow way down.*
- You were easily distracted.
- Words were hard to come by and harder to get down.
- You just wanted to *be done.*
- You wanted to do the bare minimum that was required.
- You felt frustrated.

Now consider these questions:

- What were you writing?
- To whom were you writing?
- What were you thinking about as you wrote?

Next, think back to a time when you were really engaged and motivated and maybe even *enjoyed* the writing experience. When I've discussed these scenarios with teachers and when I've reflected on these experiences in my own life, I've also found some commonalities:

- Time flew by.
- Words flowed fairly easily.
- You loved the words you wrote (or you at least felt confident in them).
- You felt like you were in the zone or experiencing flow.

Consider these questions:

- What were you writing?
- To whom were you writing?
- What were you thinking about as you wrote?

Did you notice anything interesting? Might you, depending on your purpose, audience, and mindset, sometimes look quite a bit like the "reluctant writers" in your classroom?

Several months ago, I was sitting at the dinner table with my husband and two sons, ages twelve and ten. We munched on tacos, scolded the dog for begging, and chatted about our day. After we listened to the latest about football practice, math homework, and recess, the conversation shifted to my day.

"I had a phone call with my editor," I said. "I have got to get going on this book."

My older son looked at me, surprised. "You're writing another book?" he asked. "What's this one about?"

"It's about what teachers can do when they think kids don't like to write or are doing whatever they can to avoid writing."

He looked me square in the eye, smiled, and said, "Oh! It's a book about *you*!"

Confession time. You'll know that I'm supposed to be writing simply by looking inside my refrigerator. If my fridge is clean, organized, and sanitized, you can bet that I am supposed to be writing.

Writing deadlines have this mysterious and almost magical way of reminding me that I should probably change the sheets in the guest room, organize my sock drawer, make my yearly dentist appointment, or . . . clean the fridge.

This brings me to the first of a few truths I want to share with you before we jump into the book. These truths can help us shift our perspective a bit when it comes to kids who might seem reluctant.

Truth: *All Writers Are Reluctant*

Don Murray, the father of so much of the great thinking and work around writing and teaching writing, once wrote,

> Even the most productive writers are expert dawdlers, doers of unnecessary errands, seekers of interruptions—trials to their wives or husbands, friends, associates, and themselves. They sharpen well-pointed pencils and go out to buy more blank paper, rearrange offices, wander through libraries and bookstores, chop wood, walk, drive, make unnecessary calls, nap, daydream, and try not "consciously" to think about what they are going to write so they can think subconsciously about it. (1978, 375–76)

All writers are reluctant.

OK, maybe not *all* writers are reluctant *all* of the time. But most writers I know have moments when they are less than enthused about writing—moments when they'd rather clean the fridge than try to put some sentences down on paper.

If we can embrace the fact that, at some point, all writers experience reluctance, it might help us approach those dawdlers in our classroom with a little bit of empathy and understanding rather than judgment.

Truth: *The Reasons for Reluctance Are Varied*

Curious about my own writing reluctance and habit of cleaning the fridge when I should be writing, I once jotted down a list of all the reasons I tend to avoid writing. (Confession: Writing this *list* seemed easier than doing the *actual* writing I had scheduled to do that day.)

Here are some of my reasons:

1. **Self-doubt**. I worry that I don't have anything worthwhile to say. I worry that my writing won't sound writerly enough. I doubt that I can form a complete sentence and a valuable thought for another human being.

2. **Fear**. Hot on the heels of self-doubt comes fear. Sometimes, when I sit down to write, I am overcome with it. Will I be judged for my writing? What if my grammar is way off? What if someone whom I respect disagrees with what I've written?

3. **It's hard.** Writing is hard work. It requires keen focus, deep concentration, and discipline. As one of my mentors put it, "Writing is simply this: discipline and struggle."

4. **It's time-consuming**. Writing a chapter takes days—weeks even. Cleaning the fridge or changing the sheets takes twenty minutes, tops.

5. **It's never done, it's just due.** I could fiddle with one piece of writing for the rest of my life and never really feel done. There's always more I could say, revisions I could make, things I could clarify. There simply comes a time when the piece is due, and I let it go. Tasks like organizing my sock drawer or cleaning out a closet have a definite end.

What about you? If you think back to a time when you were less than enthused to write, what would be on your list? Maybe your list would have some of the same reasons I mentioned. Or maybe your list would be different. Maybe you weren't invested in the topic. Or maybe you weren't given any choice of topic, form, or length.

My point here is that each writer is unique. We all carry with us our own reasons for reluctance. The writers in our classrooms have their reasons, too. Perhaps we should *ask* them about their reasons. Their lists might give us insight into how to best help them.

Truth: *There Are Strategies That Support* All *Writers*

The strategies I share in this book are helpful for all kids because all kids are writers, and

- all writers experience reluctance from time to time.
- all writers benefit from exposure to the quality writing of other writers.
- all writers benefit from teachers who make their thinking transparent so that they can see how another writer gets an idea from their head to the paper.
- all writers benefit from a safe space and a daily time in which they can write.
- all writers benefit from opportunities to write for real readers outside of the classroom.
- all writers grow and develop and maybe even blossom when we give them choice, keep conventions in their proper place, and assess in ways that help them to shape a positive writing identity.

Truth: *Kids Have Their Own Bag of Tricks*

Over the years, I've tried a lot of different things when I've gotten stuck or felt reluctant about my writing. Here are some of my techniques:

- **Just start writing.** The hardest part is often just getting going. Once I start, I'm often pleasantly surprised to discover that this writing thing isn't so bad after all.

- **Look at mentor books or read mentor authors.** When I'm feeling stuck on how to structure something like an acknowledgments page (or . . . ahem . . . an opening chapter to a book), I look to see how others have structured one. I'm not closely examining *what* they are saying but rather *how* they are saying it or how they are structuring it.

- **Take a short walk.** There's something about fresh air, movement, and relative quiet that helps energize me and helps me refocus. (Bonus: My dog loves it.)

- **Talk to myself about my topic.** Personally, I find it oh so easy to talk and oh so hard to write sometimes. So, I walk around my house or around the block or around the neighborhood and simply talk about the topic I'm writing about. Sometimes I record my thoughts using the voice memo on my phone. Sometimes I simply talk to myself.

- **Talk to someone else.** I call a friend, or call my editor, or talk to my husband about where I'm stuck. Sometimes just talking about the challenge helps. Other times, talking about my topic gives me the actual words I need to reengage in the work.

- **Set a timer and write without stopping.** I use the timer on my stove rather than the timer on my phone. (Phones = distraction.) I set the timer for a chunk of time (maybe thirty minutes) and I write without stopping. I tell myself, "It's OK if the writing is bad. You can revise it. Just get something down."

I recently worked with writers in first grade, third grade, and fifth grade. In each classroom, I asked the students the same question: *What do you do when you get stuck as a writer?* I asked the kids to share their thinking with a partner and then listened as the room erupted with chatter.

As I listened in and jotted down what I heard on chart paper, I noticed that the responses were strikingly similar across grade levels (and strikingly similar to some of my own tricks).

Some kids said that they take a break. They get a drink, they take a walk around the classroom, or they sit and think. Others said that they talk to someone else about their topic. A few students said that they go to the classroom library and take a moment or two to read something that is written in the same genre in which they are writing.

I encourage you to try this with your group of learners. Listen in and jot down what you hear. Just *talking* about this problem that all writers face from time to time is empowering. For me, it was helpful to read Don Murray's words about writers being dawdlers. It made me feel less shame about my own habits and more hopeful that I could find ways to help myself. This may be true for kids, too.

Truth: *Students Mirror the Enthusiasm in Our Teaching*

Recently, a group of teachers and I observed another teacher. We sat in her room for forty-five minutes and watched her teach a writing lesson, confer with individual students, and bring the kids back together at the end to reflect on the learning.

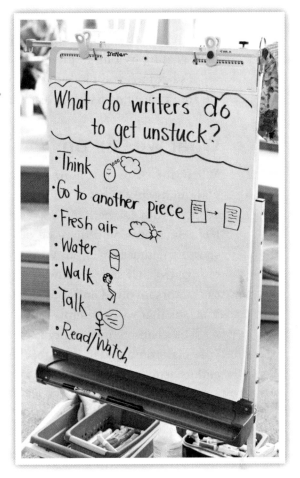

I record the ideas that students share. We can continue to add ideas to the chart throughout the year.

When the experience was over, one of the teachers who had observed the lesson exclaimed, "*I'm* ready to write! Just watching her made me want to write!"

The rest of us nodded. We had the same response. Throughout this teacher's lesson, we found ourselves smiling because *the teacher* was smiling. Two words kept coming to my mind as I watched her: *joyfully literate*. Throughout the whole experience, the teacher simply beamed. She was modeling for her students what it looked like to be a joyfully literate human being. You couldn't help but be drawn into the joy of writing because her whole demeanor invited you to do so.

Don't get me wrong. I'm not saying that we need to turn cartwheels or entertain as we teach. Simply *smiling* while we teach might help kids engage with writing in a more positive way.

It's hard to expect kids to engage in writing with joy, purpose, and energy if we aren't engaging with the teaching of writing with joy, purpose, and energy.

What We Can Do

When any of us is required to write without a strong sense of purpose, without a sense of ownership of a piece, or to an audience whom we do not connect with (or perhaps do not even have a clear conception of), we can feel reluctant. Could there be other factors at work when students are not showing enthusiasm about writing in our classrooms, factors that are beyond our control? Of course. However, we have at least some control over many of the factors involved and total control over some of them. This is good news; it means that we can help!

The chapters in this book lay out six practical ways to make shifts in your classroom and in your teaching to help students write with energy and enthusiasm:

1. Use mentors and modeling to fuel engagement.
2. Create a safe and daily space for writing.
3. Expose writers to real readers.
4. Offer choice.
5. Maintain a healthy perspective on conventions.
6. Shape writing identity through assessment.

In the following chapters, you'll notice some consistent features:

- **An invitation to reflect.** In each chapter, I'll invite you to pause and consider how the chapter's topic looks or how you might experience it in your own life as a writer.

- **A look inside the classroom.** Here, you'll see what this strategy looks like in real teachers' classrooms. You'll see photographs and samples of kids' work so that you can get a clear picture in your mind of what the strategy looks like in real life.

- **A reality check.** Standards are a reality for many of us in classrooms today. In this section, we'll turn our attention to how to the strategies and ideas in this work support state and national standards.

- **Practical ideas to put to use.** In every chapter, I'll share some small and powerful ways to try out the strategy in your own classroom. My hope is that you will see a few ideas you can try right away! We'll explore how you can use real-world examples, along with modeling your own thinking and writing, to help kids approach writing with enthusiasm. I'll also help you think about what the strategy might look like when you are working with students one-on-one.

- **Questions for reflection.** While the guidance in this book is based on experiences in many classrooms across the country, the most important classroom for you to consider in your reading is your own. At the end of each chapter, you'll find some questions to ponder when thinking about your own classroom.

So, let's get started!

Chapter Two

Use Mentors and Modeling to Fuel Engagement

Many teachers find that when they do more and better modeling—writing for and with their students—everything improves: kids' engagement, abundance of ideas for writing, willingness to write and take risks, knowledge of how and what to write, and the quality and quantity of their writing.

—Regie Routman, *Writing Essentials*

I recently purchased a blanket scarf. If you are fortunate enough to live in a place where blanket scarves are not necessary for winter survival, I'll help you out here. A blanket scarf, as the name suggests, is a square-shaped scarf that is so large that it could be used as an actual blanket. Well, truth be told, it's only big enough to serve as a blanket for a child, but you get the idea. I had seen several of my friends wear them during last year's oh-so-long, really never-ending winter, and I loved how cozy yet stylish they looked.

I was tickled with my purchase (eight dollars on clearance!) and was so excited to try it out! However, once I got home with the scarf, reality set in.

How on earth could I *wear* this thing? It was huge!

May I pause for a brief moment to give thanks for the fact we live in the age of the internet? With just a few clicks of the mouse, my laptop led me to a website that provided a straightforward, simple procedure to help me. I should begin by folding the scarf into a triangle (easy enough) and then I should tie the ends behind my neck (Which ones?). Then I could let the material hang (Which part? Where is this hanging?), or I could move the point to my shoulder (Wait, on my shoulder? Hanging below my shoulder? And which point did they mean, exactly?).

After several frustrating attempts to wrangle the scarf, I started fishing around in my purse for the receipt. "Forget it," I thought. "I'll just return it." The excitement I felt when I purchased the scarf was long, long gone. In its place, I felt frustration, bewilderment, and discouragement. "How do my friends do it?" I wondered.

Just as I located the receipt, a thought occurred to me. The explanation I had read was helpful, but what I really needed was for someone to *show* me how to take charge of this incredibly large chunk of fabric.

Back to the internet I went, this time in search of a video or two that might be of help. In 0.31 seconds, my computer pulled up no less than 48,600 video clips showing more than a dozen ways to wear a blanket scarf. Voilà!

As I watched the video clips—pausing and replaying particular segments as needed—I thought of something I had heard a teacher say many years ago: "A demonstration is more powerful than a description."

The description of how to tie my blanket scarf was only marginally helpful. Once I encountered difficulty, my fixed-mindset brain was ready to throw in the towel (or the scarf, in this case). It was the video clips of someone *demonstrating* how to tie the scarf that helped me to reengage, gain some confidence, and keep trying.

Apparently, I'm not the only one who finds demonstrations helpful when learning something new. A recent survey conducted by the Pew Research Center found that "roughly half of YouTube users say the platform is very important for helping them figure out how to do things they've never done before" (Smith, Toor, and van Kessel 2018, 2).

I wonder if writers in our classrooms experience something similar to what I experienced with my blanket scarf. Perhaps, at some point in their lives, they started out as enthusiastic and energetic writers—or, at least, they were enthusiastic and energetic about the *idea* of writing. But, as challenges arose (as they always do in writing), I wonder if they started to lose the spark and the resiliency to stick it out, persevere, and push through. And I wonder if, like me, they might benefit from someone coming alongside them and *showing* them how to wrangle their thoughts into writing.

Reflect on Modeling in Your Own Life and in Your Own Writing

Let's take a moment to reflect on your own life. I'm guessing that demonstrations have played an important role in how you've learned lots of things—from changing a tire, to practicing yoga, to becoming a teacher, to learning how to make the perfect piecrust.

When you set out to learn something new, maybe you pulled a book off the shelf or pulled up some instructions on a website. But I'm guessing that what was most helpful to you was watching an expert *demonstrate* how to do it. I'm guessing that this demonstration was more powerful than the description and it helped the new skill seem much more doable. Am I right?

Now let's pivot and think about what happens in your own life as a writer.

Imagine for a moment that you've been asked to write a letter of recommendation for a student teacher or a colleague. Chances are, before you begin, you'll take a look at other letters of recommendation so that you can see how they're structured, what the form is like, and what kind of language is typically included. These examples of letters of recommendation, or mentor texts, will give you some ideas of how you might write your own letter. They'll be helpful.

But, once you begin to actually write, I'm guessing that will break down a bit. You have the mentor text—you know what it should look like when all is said and done—but you haven't actually watched someone write a letter of recommendation in front of you. You haven't seen another writer wrestle with wording and phrasing and paragraphing. So, while the mentor text is helpful, it's missing something. It's missing the demonstration.

Think of it this way: A mentor text is like the picture on the top of the box of a jigsaw puzzle. It shows what the puzzle should look like when it's complete. But modeling, or teacher demonstration, goes a step beyond. When an expert puzzle completer (in keeping with this analogy) shows you how he looks carefully at each piece, how he finds the border pieces, and how he looks for pieces that have a similar color scheme, you are able to see *how* an expert puts the puzzle together to create the finished product that is depicted on the box.

As writing teachers, part of our job is to inspire all students to see what's possible in their own writing by introducing them to the powerful, high-quality writing of others that can be found in mentor texts. But we also need to take that next step and *demonstrate* how a writer gets an idea from his or her head to the page.

What Does This Look Like in the Classroom?

It's a blustery Monday morning in Whitney Fridley's kindergarten classroom. I've been invited in to teach the kids how to add labels to their drawings. When I arrive, the kids scurry to the carpet area in front of a large easel with chart paper and a stool for the teacher. I take a seat, and together we look at a few pages from some nonfiction books I've brought in from the public library. I show them how these published authors—writers just like them—have carefully labeled certain pictures. Together, we talk about what these labels do to support us as readers.

After a few minutes, I shift the focus. I tell the kids that I've been working on a piece of writing about cooking, a topic on which I'm becoming an expert. (My own kids have come to expect that I will feed them each and every day.) The kids watch as I create a drawing of my oven, some pots and pans, and my spice rack. I add some labels to my drawing, thinking aloud as I consider what might be most helpful to my reader.

My modeled writing of a sketch with labels

I release the kids to gather their writing materials and begin writing. As I walk around the classroom, I notice that all of the kids have begun to draw and write. When I settle in next to Hank, I see that he's finished his drawing of a tractor and is carefully labeling all of the different parts.

Another student has sketched a football field (as well as a majority of the Minnesota Vikings football players) and is adding the word *touchdown* to the space above his drawing

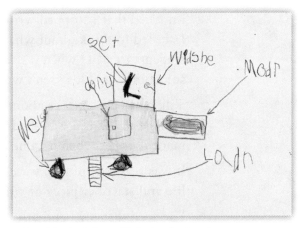

Hank's sketch and labels of a tractor

of the end zone. I come alongside another student, who has chosen to write about how to take care of a dog. Together, we take another look at the labeled pictures from the books I brought, and we talk about the labels she might add to help her readers.

After the lesson, the teacher and I marvel at how quickly the students invested their heart and energy into their writing and at how excited the kids were to share their progress with a partner at the end of the lesson. We both agree that the teacher modeling contributed to this.

Being the Writer Your Students Need You to Be

Go Forth and Write

Recently, I invited a group of elementary teachers to do some writing. I asked each of them to write about a school memory that had affected him or her. The teachers watched as I reflected on my own memories, chose one, and began to write about it. Then I asked them to do the same. After a few minutes of thinking and chatter, we all settled in and began writing.

About ten minutes later, I asked the teachers to pause from their writing and talk about the experience. "What supported you as a writer? What was challenging? Did you learn anything about yourself as a writer?"

As the teachers reflected with a partner, I listened in.

- "I noticed that I stopped writing every now and then just because I needed to think about what to say next. I'm always telling my students to write when it's writing time, but I realize now that sometimes my kids aren't writing because they are thinking."

- "Talking to my partner about the memory first helped a lot. As I talked about it, I was kind of organizing my thoughts, and it made it easier when it came time to write."

- "It was really helpful to watch Kelly choose a memory from her life and start her piece of writing before she asked us to do it."

- "I noticed that my handwriting is super sloppy, and as I was writing, I noticed that I wasn't paying much attention to things like capitals, periods, and correct spelling. I was too focused on trying to get my memory down on the page."

- "My hand was killing me after only five minutes! No wonder my kids stop every now and then."

- "It was harder than I thought it would be."

- "I love to write, so I loved this experience. But I noticed that as I was writing, I was thinking, 'Am I going to have to share this with someone else? What will they think of my writing?'"

The more we write, the more insight we gain into what students experience and the more we understand the subject matter of writing. Think about it: We don't sign our kids up to take piano lessons from someone who doesn't play the piano himself. People who play the piano tend to make better piano teachers because they actually engage in the skill they are teaching.

To be genuinely helpful writing models for our kids, we need to be writers. We need to climb into the trenches ourselves. Don't worry. I'm not suggesting that you write America's next great novel or that you spend your next free weekend crafting a research paper.

There are dozens of ways to engage in writing. Here are a few ideas you might consider:

- Keep a gratitude journal. Each day, jot down a few things for which you are grateful.

- Write notes of appreciation to your principal, fellow teachers, and support staff.

- Digitally, or by hand, create a photo book for your children, your partner, your students, or yourself. Write a caption for each photo that captures the memory.

- Write a blog post about teaching, cooking, cycling, or any other area of passion. Publish it or simply hold on to it.

- Take sketchnotes (visual notes) at your next professional development session or staff meeting.

- Participate in a Twitter chat.

- Write an online review of a new restaurant, a book you've read, or a product you've recently purchased.

- Write love notes to your significant other and leave them in random places where he or she will find them.

- Leave supportive or reflective comments on someone else's blog.

- If you have small children of your own, keep a written record of funny things they do or say.

- Carve out ten minutes a month to write a letter to an active service member.

- When a family member celebrates a birthday, create a list of things you admire and appreciate about them—one item for each year of their age. (My husband's grandfather recently celebrated his one-hundredth birthday. Over several days, I wrote a list of 100 things I admired about him. When he read them, he cried.)

- At the end of the school day, take a moment or two to write down your reflections and thoughts. What excited you today? What did you learn? What was frustrating or challenging?

- As you confer with your students during reading, writing, or math time, jot down a few sentences to help you remember what you talked about and what you celebrated in the students' work.

- If you and your colleagues meet in a PLC (professional learning community) or team meeting, carve out five minutes each time you meet and use that time to write down your thoughts or hopes.

Whether it's a journal, a blog, some poetry, or an article, engage in the writing process for yourself. Do it often. Then ask yourself some questions: What supported you as a writer? What was challenging? Did you learn anything about yourself as a writer? Did anyone else read your writing? How did knowing that your writing would (or wouldn't) have an audience affect you as a writer?

If you do this kind of work outside the writing classroom, you'll be better equipped to support, guide, teach, and energize the students in front of you.

Reality Check: *Standards and Rigor*

Where do mentor texts and teacher demonstration fit in the ever-increasing presence of local, state, and national standards? In my opinion, both of them fit right smack-dab in the middle of all of it.

As I read through the Common Core State Standards (NGA Center for Best Practices and CCSSO 2010), I notice that a particular phrase is repeated throughout the writing standards for every grade from kindergarten through fifth grade. As you skim the standards listed on page 21, see if you can pick it out.

Did you see it?

The phrase "with guidance and support from adults" is embedded in multiple standards at every grade level.

To me, this repeated phrase is a call for teachers to do more than merely assign writing or explain how to write. It's an invitation for teachers to dig deep and *show* students how a writer thinks, plans, collaborates, drafts, edits, and revises. In short, these standards (and most state standards) ask teachers to serve as writing mentors and coaches.

Think back again to a time you learned how to do something new. More specifically, think back to a time you felt truly "guided and supported" as you learned something new. Chances are it involved more than someone *telling* you what to do. Someone probably came alongside you and *showed* you what to do. They peeled back the curtain and let you observe the process behind the scenes.

Kindergarten

CCSS.ELA-LITERACY.W.K.5 "With guidance and support from adults, respond to questions and suggestions from peers and add details to strengthen writing as needed."

CCSS.ELA-LITERACY.W.K.6 "With guidance and support from adults, explore a variety of digital tools to produce and publish writing, including in collaboration with peers."

CCSS.ELA-LITERACY.W.K.8 "With guidance and support from adults, recall information from experiences or gather information from provided sources to answer a question."

First Grade

CCSS.ELA-LITERACY.W.1.5 "With guidance and support from adults, focus on a topic, respond to questions and suggestions from peers, and add details to strengthen writing as needed."

CCSS.ELA-LITERACY.W.1.6 "With guidance and support from adults, use a variety of digital tools to produce and publish writing, including in collaboration with peers."

Second Grade

CCSS.ELA-LITERACY.W.2.5 "With guidance and support from adults and peers, focus on a topic and strengthen writing as needed by revising and editing."

CCSS.ELA-LITERACY.W.2.6 "With guidance and support from adults, use a variety of digital tools to produce and publish writing, including in collaboration with peers."

Third Grade

CCSS.ELA-LITERACY.W.3.4 "With guidance and support from adults, produce writing in which the development and organization are appropriate to task and purpose."

CCSS.ELA-LITERACY.W.3.5 "With guidance and support from peers and adults, develop and strengthen writing as needed by planning, revising, and editing."

CCSS.ELA-LITERACY.W.3.6 "With guidance and support from adults, use technology to produce and publish writing (using keyboarding skills) as well as to interact and collaborate with others."

Fourth Grade

CCSS.ELA-LITERACY.W.4.5 "With guidance and support from peers and adults, develop and strengthen writing as needed by planning, revising, and editing."

CCSS.ELA-LITERACY.W.4.6 "With some guidance and support from adults, use technology, including the Internet, to produce and publish writing as well as to interact and collaborate with others; demonstrate sufficient command of keyboarding skills to type a minimum of one page in a single sitting."

Fifth Grade

CCSS.ELA-LITERACY.W.5.5 "With guidance and support from peers and adults, develop and strengthen writing as needed by planning, revising, editing, rewriting, or trying a new approach."

CCSS.ELA-LITERACY.W.5.6 "With some guidance and support from adults, use technology, including the Internet, to produce and publish writing as well as to interact and collaborate with others; demonstrate sufficient command of keyboarding skills to type a minimum of two pages in a single sitting."

Student writers are much more engaged to do the hard work that writing requires when they receive a steady diet of guidance and support from another writer.

My friend, that writer is *you*.

How Can We Give Students Opportunities to See Another Writer at Work?

How can we tap into the immense power of modeling and teacher demonstration in the classroom? How can our words and actions give students who appear to be reluctant the inspiration and tools they need to reengage and rediscover a passion for writing?

Following are several ways to make your thinking and writing visible to students. Each can help disengaged writers (and all writers) rediscover their voice, their enthusiasm, and their confidence.

Plan What You Will Model

When we model effectively, we let students see us doing honest-to-goodness real work, not delivering a practiced, polished performance. However, effective modeling *is* tailored to the specific skills and students you're working with. Here are a few questions I consider when planning writing lessons that tap into the power of mentors and modeling.

- **What kind of writing am I asking my students to do?** Am I asking students to craft a persuasive letter or an editorial? Are they going to be creating a travel brochure? Am I inviting them to contribute an article to our parent newsletter? Or am I asking them to do a deep dive into a particular moment from their lives in the form of a narrative? The kind of writing I'm asking my students to do will inform the kind of modeling I'll do and the types of mentor texts I'll use.

  For example, if students will be creating their own travel brochures, I'll want to bring in professionally published travel brochures for us to examine. (You can get these free at airports and hotels.) If my students are going to be crafting a book review, we'll immerse ourselves in this kind of writing by reading samples of published reviews.

Likewise, my modeling will need to focus on the particular kind of writing students will be doing. If students are going to be focusing on a moment in time to write a narrative piece, they'll watch me think aloud and write a bit of my own narrative.

- **What element of this kind of writing have I noticed my students struggling with?** If I've noticed that many students have researched and collected pages of facts but are now struggling to find a way to turn those facts into running text that is organized and interesting, I will definitely want to model how I organize my facts into categories or how I plan where to include these facts by creating headings. If my emergent writers are doing a lot of drawing but not a lot of writing, I might demonstrate how I add labels to my drawings to give my reader more information. My rule of thumb is this: If I notice that 40–50 percent of my students are struggling with the same skill, I plan a whole-group lesson. If it's just a few kids who need support, I can work with them one-on-one or in a small group.

- **How can I choose a topic for my modeling?** If you model a piece of writing with the same topic, purpose, and audience as your students, your attempt to show students how the process of writing works might instead be misinterpreted as the "right" way to write that particular piece. Imagine this: You, the teacher, ask students to write a persuasive letter to the principal about the need for more recess time. When you craft your letter, which you uphold as a model, on the same topic to the same audience, your students might be faced with unnecessary, distracting dilemmas: "If the teacher wrote hers in that structure, isn't that the *best* structure? Do I dare deviate from it? What if I disagree with the points the teacher made in her letter? Or what if I agree with all of them—is it OK to have the same points? Do I need to make up other ones because she's already written them? Should I just copy what she did?" None of these questions helps writers or leads to better, more authentic writing.

Instead, consider choosing topics for your modeling that will support your students. For example, if I want my fourth graders to choose a state and then write a travel brochure for that state, I could ask them to make their selections and then, once all of my students have selected, I could choose a state that hasn't been chosen by anyone else. Now my teacher-created writing won't be an exact match for the writing that my students will be doing. Or, if I'm asking first graders to create an informational poster meant to teach a reader about a topic, I'll likely choose a topic such as "driving in the snow" or "creating a monthly menu" or "cleaning and organizing your refrigerator"—a topic that students aren't likely to choose for themselves—so that I can model the process and my thinking without encroaching on their topics.

- **What kind of language can I use to make the invisible process of writing visible to my students?** If I'm not thinking aloud before I write and as I write, then students are simply watching my pen move across the page. So, as I plan, I consider how I can crack open my thinking and let students see what's going on inside my head. As I plan, I think about including phrases such as these:

  - *I'm thinking . . .*
  - *I'm wondering . . .*
  - *I'm not sure if . . .*
  - *As I reread this, I'm thinking . . .*
  - *I could write . . .*
  - *I could say it this way . . .*
  - *I may come back and rework this . . .*

- **What mentor texts will I use?** When choosing a mentor text to use in a particular lesson, I find it helpful to do the following:

  - **Decide what I am looking to illustrate with the mentor text.** For example, am I teaching students how to include headings in their nonfiction pieces? Do I want to show them how to craft an ending that brings closure? Do I want students to think about paragraphing?

- **Dive into books.** These might be books that I've already flagged for a particular craft move I've noticed, books that are written by authors who I know are strong writers, or books that my students have recommended to me in general.

If, once you start looking in books, you can't find the craft move or skill you are looking for, it's a good idea to stop and think! If strong writers aren't using this skill or craft move often enough for you to find it, you might want to question whether it is worth teaching.

Show Kids How You Lean on the Work of Other Writers

One of the ways that we can maximize the power of teacher demonstration and modeling is to show students how we ourselves rely on the work of other writers to bring energy and engagement to our own writing.

Think back to earlier in this chapter when you imagined that you'd been asked to write a letter of recommendation for a student teacher or colleague. I suggested that most of us, when asked to do this kind of writing, first look at other samples of letters of recommendation to help us think about how the letter might be structured and what kinds of information is usually included. In other words, before we write, we typically lean on the work of other writers.

Most writers I know routinely look to the work of others before they begin their own writing. Are you writing a wedding or baby announcement? Chances are you'll look at dozens of examples to help you out. Are you updating your résumé or crafting a cover letter? Likely, you'll peruse other résumés and cover letters before attending to your own.

When you think aloud and write in front of your students, making the invisible process visible, it's only natural to include this part of the process.

For example, if you're teaching students how writers conclude their persuasive letters, you might show them how you look carefully at the way other writers end their letters and use that information to help you craft your own.

If you're teaching your emergent writers how to add labels to their pictures, you might showcase a few published books that utilize this feature.

If you are going to draw from the work of other writers, you'll want to have a collection of rich and varied texts from which to choose. If you don't have access to a large classroom library or if you're in the beginning stages of growing your classroom library, consider borrowing books from your school and public libraries. Show students the deep reverence and respect you have for books and for the people who write them.

For example, I might show students the first page of the book *Coral Reefs*, by Seymour Simon. After reading the page aloud, I can go back and call attention to a specific craft move that Seymour is using (e.g., using the word *you* to speak directly to the reader). I can ask students to think about and consider what that particular craft move does for them as a reader. They'll likely discover that when an author speaks to the reader, it pulls the reader in and makes the text more interesting.

After we've had a chance to examine what this writer has done, I can show students how I emulate, not imitate, this craft move in my own writing. I don't need to be writing about coral reefs; I could be writing about anything: tsunamis or the American Revolution or the Underground Railroad or gun control. As I write, I can make my thinking visible to students by saying something like: *One of the things I noticed Seymour doing in his writing was using the word* you *and speaking directly to the reader. Let me try that in my own writing. You know that I've been working on this informative piece about growing tomatoes. Watch me as I try using the word* you *and speaking directly to my reader. I could write, "Once you've transplanted the small tomato plant, you'll want to make sure the plant stays toasty warm during the cool spring nights. Surround your growing plant with a wall of water (found at most plant stores)."*

Or, my students and I could take a closer look at Melvin Berger's book *Why Do Feet Smell?* In this book, Melvin utilizes a unique organizational structure: he asks a question, he answers the question in short form, and then he elaborates on the answer to the question. The elaboration of the answer is the part of the text where Melvin Berger teaches his reader more about the topic.

After we explored the text together, I could show students how I can use that same organizational structure in my own writing, regardless of the topic. For example, I might be writing an informational piece on the Lewis and Clark expedition. My modeling might look something like this: *I noticed that one of the ways that Melvin Berger structures his writing is in a question-and-answer format. Let me try that with this piece that I've been working on about the bullboats that Lewis and Clark used. I could write a question like, "Did people in the Lewis and Clark expedition use boats to cross the Missouri?" Then, I could give my reader a short answer: "Yes." Next, I could do what I saw Melvin Berger do and use the next section of text to tell my reader more. I think I'll say, "Sergeant Pryor and Privates Shannon, Hall, and Windsor made bullboats out of sticks and animal hides, just as they had seen Hidatsa and Mandan tribes do. Bullboats were small, bowl-shaped boats that kept the crew and supplies stable, even in the rough waters of the Yellowstone River and Missouri River."*

Mentors are in service of the modeling. When a teacher specifically models how he or she pulls inspiration or structure or craft moves from another writer, it makes the writing process less mystical and vague and helps students learn how to lean on mentor texts to help strengthen and enliven their own writing.

Write in Front of Kids

Let's be clear from the get-go. There is a difference between *explaining* and *modeling*. There's an important distinction to be made between telling and showing.

When you create a piece of writing on your own, show it to your students, and then tell them how you wrote it, you are *explaining*. Modeling is different. When you model, you make the invisible process of writing visible for your students. In other words, you think and write in the moment—off the cuff—in front of your students. As you do this, you show them all that goes into putting your thoughts and ideas down on paper.

Modeling doesn't require you to write perfectly. When you write in front of your kids, you're not modeling perfection; you're modeling process. You're showing them how you think, plan, make decisions, cross things out, change your mind, revise, and persevere. You're showing them how writers write.

As you write in front of your students, you think aloud and lift the veil so that your students can see that writing can sometimes be challenging for everyone. This peek into the real world of writing helps students be better prepared when things become challenging in their own writing.

Think Aloud as You Make a Myriad of Decisions

When I first started making my thinking and writing visible to my students, I did most of the thinking and decision-making in my lesson plan book. I made all of my choices (such as choosing my topic and planning out my writing) behind the scenes so that when I sat down to "teach" my students how to write, I wouldn't look like a fool—in other words, so that I would look like I knew what I was doing.

I now realize that the most important part of teaching writing was the part I was doing when the students weren't even there! All the choices I made as a writer needed to be visible to my students. In other words, when we model, we make what is invisible—namely all of choices we make—visible. When we crack open our thinking and make all of those choices *in front of our students*, we demystify the writing process, which helps make writing seem more doable.

So now, when I plan writing lessons, I plan with careful precision the skill or behavior or craft move that I'm hoping to teach. However, I don't try to plan the choices I'll need to make as a writer. I want students to see (and learn from) all of the choices I make as I'm writing in front of them.

For example, if I'm planning a lesson on how to write a powerful introduction for a nonfiction piece, I'll carefully plan which mentor texts I'll use to show students how other writers begin. I'll place a bookmark on the specific pages ahead of time so that I can turn to them quickly when I'm ready to teach. I'll also think about and prepare the anchor chart I might create. I'll write a title for the anchor chart: *How do other writers begin their pieces?* I know that, during the lesson, my students and I will work together to record the various ways that our mentor authors begin their writing.

I'll plan these parts of the lesson (the mentor texts I'll use and the anchor chart we'll use to record our thinking) carefully and precisely so that I won't waste precious moments in the classroom.

However, when it comes time to think about and write my own introduction, I'll deliberately *not* plan ahead. I want students to see me think and make some decisions in real time. My modeling might sound something like this: *Writers, each of us has chosen a topic that we know well and feel that we could teach someone about. You know that I have chosen to write about basketball. Watch me as I use what we've learned from other authors and think about how I'll begin my piece. Maybe I'll start by speaking to my reader and asking questions, like we saw one of the mentor authors do. I could write: "Do you love hanging out with your friends while getting some exercise?" Or I could say, "Are you looking for something fun to do this weekend? Look no further! Basketball might just be the adventure you are looking for!" Or I could try what we saw another author do. She set the scene and used some sound words to pull the reader in. Let me try that: "Dribble, dribble, dribble, shoot, and SWOOSH! There's nothing quite as exhilarating as seeing a basketball fly through the hoop." I think I like the second one. Watch as I get those words down on the page.*

Demonstrate How You Engage in Productive Struggle

A couple of years ago, I heard someone bemoan the negative impact of social media on our emotional well-being. He said, "We compare other people's 'highlight reels' with our 'behind the scenes.'" We see the picture-perfect images on Instagram or Twitter or Facebook and we compare them with our everyday, mundane, and often not-so-picture-perfect lives.

If we're not careful, mentor texts can trip up the writers in our classroom in the same way that social media can trip us up. These students see the finished product—the polished work of another writer—but they don't see the struggle that went into creating the piece of writing. One of the most important things that modeling accomplishes is that it shows students the behind-the-scenes process of writing.

Many students (and adults) believe a sort of fairy tale that goes like this: When "expert" writers sit down to write, some sort of writing fairy sprinkles them with a magic pixie dust and words simply fly out from their fingertips.

Any "expert" writer will tell you that is *not* how it goes. Writing is often a muddled mix of discipline and struggle.

When we demonstrate or model our own thinking for students, we take off the mask and allow our students to see us engage in that discipline and struggle.

If we don't show students that struggling is actually part of the process, we do them a great disservice. If we make our writing look consistently easy, our students will inevitably melt when they go off to write independently and encounter the challenges that await most writers. We need to show them the kind of resiliency that writers develop as they work through these challenges.

So, let down your guard and let students see the authentic process that's going on in your mind. Be transparent and let them bear witness to the struggle. Your teacher-created writing samples don't need to be picture-perfect. Instead, show students how you cross out words or phrases, circle words that you'd like to come back to later to check the spelling, or use arrows to move whole sections of text around. These pieces of teacher-created writing should show the tracks of your thinking and process rather than perfection.

Here are a few examples of what productive struggle might sound like:

- *Writers, we're continuing to work on writing the text for our travel brochures. You know that I'm creating a brochure on Glacier National Park. I've chosen the first two places I want to highlight in my brochure: Lake McDonald Lodge and Logan Pass Visitor Center. Today, I'm struggling to figure out what other parts of this national park I want to tell my reader about. There are so many special places in the park! I know that, in a travel brochure, I'll want to include just a few so that I don't overwhelm my reader. Watch me as I think through this challenge.*

  One of the things I'm thinking I'll include is something about the hiking that you can do in Glacier National Park. But hiking is such a big topic to include in my brochure! In my research, I discovered that there are over seven hundred hiking trails in Glacier. I'm wondering, should I write about hiking in the park in general, or should I highlight a particular hike? I think I'll go back to the professional brochures that we looked at a few days ago to see how they are structured.

  I'm noticing that, in these brochures, the author provides an interesting heading and then tells a little bit more about the topic. Maybe I could write the heading "Breathtaking Hiking Trails," or maybe the heading could be "More Than Seven Hundred Trails to Explore." Then, in that section, I could say something like, "Whether you are new to hiking or are ready to tackle backcountry hiking and camping, Glacier National Park has a trail for you!"

- *I've been working on this section of my biography of Chief Joseph for a while now. It's just not coming together. I think I'll leave this paragraph for now and come back to it. Sometimes it helps me approach my writing challenges with fresh eyes if I give myself a break from the part that is challenging.*

- *I'm starting a new narrative piece today about the big snowstorm we had last week and how my whole neighborhood was covered in white. I could start by saying something like, "The morning broke cold and bright." Hmm . . . that's OK. Maybe I could say, "When I opened my eyes on that cold morning in December, the first thing I saw was blue sky and white snow." I'm not happy with that sentence either. I think, for now, I'll just write one of them down. I can always come back to this section later and change it. Sometimes something comes to me while I'm writing another part of my narrative.*

- *Writers, today I'm thinking about how I'll do my page layout for this section of my book about the Sonoran Desert. I'm drawing a blank! Sometimes, when I'm struggling with something like this, it helps to look at some published books to see how other writers set up their pages. Watch as I look at a few of these nonfiction books to get some ideas for my own writing.*

Give your less-than-enthused writers a glimpse into the real world of a writer. By doing so, you'll help them see that *all* writers struggle.

It's hard work.

But that's OK.

All noble endeavors are hard.

Use the Tools That Kids Are Using

When you model, it helps to mirror the same kind of writing conditions your students will have. Are the students going to be writing by hand on lined paper? If so, you'll want to write by hand on lined paper as well, perhaps using a large sheet of lined chart paper and a dark-colored marker so that all students can see. Are the kids going to be typing? If possible, use an interactive whiteboard or projection system so that kids can see *you* type up your piece.

Here's one more helpful hint: I find that, when you are modeling, it helps to have students gathered in close proximity to you and your teaching. Even in upper-elementary classrooms, students can gather together either on the floor or in chairs. When students are watching and listening to a demonstration, it helps to be close to the action and the thinking.

Keep It Short and Focused

Many teachers ask me, "Do I have to create my *whole* piece of writing in front of my students?"

No.

Keep your modeling short and focused. You don't need to teach the world of writing. Instead, focus on *one* teaching point at a time. For example, if I'm going to show my students how I use headings to organize and plan my writing, I'll resist the urge to also throw in some teaching points about capitals, periods, and paragraphing. Instead, I'll teach how to use headings to organize and plan my writing with a laser-like focus. If I teach too many things in one lesson, the writers in my classroom don't feel energized. They feel overwhelmed.

Give Students Multiple Opportunities to Talk with a Partner

Donald Graves once said, "Beginning writers show through voice alone that writing is much more of a speech event than a writing event" (quoted in Newkirk and Kittle 2013, 45).

I find that when I give students the opportunity to talk about what they are noticing and thinking, students internalize the skill that I'm teaching and they feel more confident when it comes time to do the same kind of work in their own writing. Additionally, language learners and learners who struggle are more likely to find success when they are given lots of opportunity for scaffolded conversations (Freeman and Freeman 2002; Krashen 2003).

Here are some examples of the kinds of things you might say to spur partner conversation and help writers verbally process their thinking.

- *Think for a moment. What did you notice me do as a writer? Turn and tell your partner what you noticed.*

- *Did you see how I did that? Did you see how I _____? How do you think this helped me as a writer?*

- *You watched me and listened to my thinking as I organized my writing by planning across my pages. Now, it's your turn. Tell your partner what you're planning to write on each page of your writing.*

- *Did you see how I added some dialogue to my piece? I think it really made my characters come to life! Take a moment to read your piece to yourself. Are there some places in your writing where you could add some dialogue? Talk to your partner and show them the places you're thinking you'll make your characters talk.*

- *Did you see how I tried a lot of sentences aloud before I chose the sentences I wanted to use at the beginning of my writing? Now, it's your turn. Turn to your partner and try some beginnings aloud. Don't worry about writing them down; just say them aloud for now until you hear some sentences that you might want to try in your writing.*

Many teachers find that it's helpful to have writers sit next to a "thinking partner" while they observe teacher demonstrations. If you've prepared these partnerships before the lesson, you won't waste precious moments while students try to find someone with whom to talk.

Break a Big Writing Task into Bite-Size Chunks

Let's imagine that you say, *Today, we're going to choose a cause that matters to us and then write a persuasive letter to an elected official. Our letter will contain a call to action for our cause.*

You might notice that your students' eyes start to gloss over. The task that you've just explained sounds too big and a bit overwhelming!

I've found that if you can teach (and demonstrate) one chunk at a time, it can be really helpful. For example, you might start out by modeling how *you* think about the issues that are important to *you* and settle on one that you think you could research and write about. After students have seen you engage in this work, you can release them to do the same: *OK, it's your turn. Think about the issues or causes that matter to you. Jot them down on a sticky note. You can talk to your partner as you do this—sometimes two heads are better than one! Then, choose one cause or issue that you feel you could write about.*

After students have settled on a topic, you can call them back together and show them how you decide which elected official could have the most impact on this issue or cause. For example, is this a local issue that a city council or mayor should consider, or is this something that state or federal officials might be able to do something about?

After they've seen and heard you do this work, you can release the students to tackle that particular question with their own topic in mind.

When you teach (and model) a little bit, then release, then teach and model again, you break a complex (and sometimes overwhelming) process into bite-size pieces so that it feels more manageable and doable.

How Can Coaching Help Us Maximize the Power of Mentors and Modeling?

When we think about the power of teacher modeling and demonstration in the writing classroom, we typically think that the power is coming from the demonstration itself. And it's true that demonstration is powerful, especially for students who might appear to be reluctant: it helps those students reengage with enthusiasm and confidence. But, in my opinion, part of the powerful punch of modeling comes when we coach and confer with individual writers. Because we've gone first—we've engaged in the writing experience in front of them—it gives us credibility and a unique perspective when doling out advice to other writers.

Here are a few things to consider when you are coaching writers:

- **Lean on your own experience.** When my mother-in-law gives me advice on how to prune my raspberry bushes, I listen. I listen (and usually follow her advice) because I know that my mother-in-law has grown raspberries for years and she knows what she's talking about. She has gained some credibility as a raspberry pruner with me because she's done the work herself. It's the same with writing. If you're willing to do the same hard work you're asking your students to do, I think you'll find that your students will be more receptive to your guidance and support because they'll know that you're engaging in the same work they are. You can also lean on your own experience as a writer and share the tips and tricks you've learned.

- **Offer a little grace.** As teachers, we have a special responsibility to be mindful regarding our assumptions. For example, on a hectic day, it might be easy to slip into believing that a writer is willfully disengaged or that they don't care about their writing. However, as any of us who has ever fretted over writing something—a wedding toast, a cover letter for a job application, a blog post—knows, perfectionism can also contribute to reluctance in writing. Worrying about getting it right on the page can be paralyzing.

  Grace, and a personal understanding of the difficulty of writing, can help us to see the reasons behind behaviors that might otherwise be puzzling. Several months ago, I was working in a first-grade classroom. As I walked around the room to confer with writers, a particular child caught my eye. I noticed that he wasn't writing. Instead, he was poking at the corner of his eye with the eraser of his pencil. My first thought was: "I totally understand where you are right now." In that moment, I recalled times in my own life as a writer where I was frozen or having trouble getting started or feeling disengaged or discouraged or completely unmotivated.

  I think earlier in my teaching career I might have seen that child as noncompliant or not following directions. But now that I've done a fair amount of writing myself, I am able to see that child for who he truly is: a writer who is encountering some struggle and challenge. I can come alongside him with some grace, understanding where he is in his journey as a writer instead of being annoyed that he's not doing what he's supposed to be.

  A side note here: After I gently encouraged the child to put the pencil (and eraser) down and away from his eye, I asked him to *tell* me what he wanted to say. I said, *Don't worry about writing anything down right now. Just tell* me *what you want to say.* And, not surprisingly, his words just bubbled out. At that point I could guide him by truly listening with openness and curiosity. Then I said, *Let's try to get some of those words down on the page. Think back. What was the first thing you told me?* As he repeated it, he picked up his pencil and was able to begin writing.

• **Use your own work as a mentor text.** Oftentimes when I'm working with an individual student and they feel stuck, I bring them back to the writing that I did in front of the class. I can engage in more modeling or thinking aloud (and maybe even do a little bit more writing) so they can see how a writer gets an idea from their head onto the page. Similarly, I can pull out the mentor text that I've used or another mentor text that shows the same craft move or structure that the child is struggling with and I can use that text in conjunction with the text I've written as part of my modeling to give them a little nudge in the right direction and help them reengage with their writing.

Closing Thoughts

Writing teacher, trainer, and author Vicki Spandel says, "Nothing, absolutely *nothing* you will ever do as a teacher will be more powerful than modeling writing in front of your students" (2004, 181). I couldn't agree more. Mentor texts and modeling are essential to what we do. When we show students what's possible by highlighting the work of others and then give them a peek into our own creative process, we demystify the writing process and give those less-than-enthused writers (and all writers) the guidance and support they need to persevere with energy, investment, and confidence.

I've listed some questions to consider as you take a reflective and honest look at your current practices in the hope of engaging all your students—especially those students who might appear to be reluctant.

If you're reading this book with a group of colleagues, use these questions to guide your shared conversation and learning.

Questions for Reflection

1. Am I making my thinking and writing visible to my students?

2. Am I engaging in the same kinds of writing experiences that I'm asking my students to engage in?

3. Are there multiple opportunities for my students to see the authentic struggle that all writers encounter?

4. What mentor texts can I use to highlight an element of craft or structure?

5. What kinds of writing experiences am I engaging in outside of the classroom? What ideas from this chapter might I try?

Chapter Three

Create a Safe and Daily Space for Writing

We are in the business of taking care of hearts
and looking out for the hearts of students.

—John Schumacher, speaking at the 2019 North Dakota
Literacy Association Summer Institute

Although it was years ago, my first day of student teaching is still fresh in my mind.

The mid-August morning had started off cool and crisp, but by the afternoon it was clear that summer was still putting up a fight. I was overdressed, anxious to make a good impression on Molly, my cooperating teacher. The un-air-conditioned room in Willson Elementary and my overwhelming nervousness caused little beads of sweat to appear—unwanted—on my head and face.

I walked into the bright and cheerful K–1 classroom. Immediately, I saw Molly. She was unpacking some items from a box and placing them on her desk. Right next to her desk, I noticed a small table with a gift bag on top, which was clearly marked with my name. Touched by the gesture, I relaxed and took a deep breath. When Molly noticed me, she came toward me with a wide smile and an outstretched hand. I immediately felt at ease.

For the next two weeks, I observed a master teacher at work. Molly had an air about her that energized everyone around her. I took copious notes. I shadowed her as she taught, conferred, read aloud, and took her turn at playground duty. I listened to how she spoke to children and to their families.

Slowly, over time, she handed over more of the teaching responsibilities to me. I took over the read-aloud portion of the day and then the math lesson. Molly was close at hand as I planned my lessons. She listened, encouraged, and offered sage wisdom, all the while letting me know that this was a safe place to begin learning about teaching.

"You'll make mistakes," she said one afternoon while I was fretting about the next day's science lesson. "We all do. It's part of teaching and learning. None of us are perfect at this."

As I began my weeks of solo teaching, I marveled at how *daily* this job was. Every school day, without fail, parents dropped off these little souls and every day I was given the enormous responsibility to teach, guide, and support them. The weightiness of the job was daunting. But day after day, I noticed it getting easier. Well, maybe it wasn't easier. But I began to feel more confident. I made plenty of mistakes, but Molly was always there to talk me through what I had learned and to encourage me to keep trying.

As I look back on that experience, I'm enormously grateful. I didn't realize it at the time, but now, looking back, I can see it clearly: Molly had provided me *space* to do good work and to learn.

It started with the physical space that Molly had created for me—that little table nestled in next to her desk. This was a place I could put my teacher bag and coffee, settle in after school to work on my plans, or catch my breath while the students were at recess.

The space that Molly provided went far beyond this little table. Part of the beauty of student teaching experiences is that they provide a *daily* space and a *daily* time to try things out and to practice the art of teaching. If my teaching was less than stellar today, I'd have another chance—a fresh start each day—to try again. The daily practice was powerful.

And, probably the most important space that Molly gave me was a safe emotional space. Understanding that I was a deer-in-the-headlights, brand-new-baby teacher, Molly gave me space and even a kind of permission to try things, make mistakes, learn, and try again. Through her interactions and conversations with me, it was clear that she was not expecting perfection. She only expected that I try, learn, and grow.

We humans are temperamental, fragile, and sensitive beings. When we are learning something new, like teaching, or driving, or cooking, it's helpful to have space in which to do the work of learning: physical space, schedule space, and emotional space.

This is true for us as adults.

It's also true for student writers.

If providing a safe and daily space is helpful—and maybe even necessary—for those of us who approach a situation like student teaching with enthusiasm and energy, how much more helpful (and necessary) might these kinds of spaces be for students who approach writing with less enthusiasm?

Reflect on Your Own Life as a Writer

Cast your mind back to your life as an elementary, middle school, or high school student. What were your writing experiences like? Do you look back with fondness and gratitude or does it make you cringe a bit?

If you're like some of the teachers I've talked to, your memories might consist of some combination of the following:

- lots and lots of red pen on your writing
- squirming or finding it hard to focus while sitting in a row of uncomfortable desks
- trying to fill the pages so that you could meet the page-length requirement, with little thought to the *content*
- rigid, formulaic assignments
- wishing you could talk through your ideas and challenges with a friend or peer while you were writing
- beginning a piece with excitement and attention to detail and then running out of steam as you got deeper into the writing

- feeling sheer panic rise as you realized that your deadline was looming and you were not finished

- trying to complete a writing assignment at home, but feeling somewhat lost without the support you might have had in class

- second-guessing yourself or editing yourself as you wrote

- worrying about making a small (or large) mistake in your writing and being embarrassed or called out.

Whether you can remember your own writing experiences as a student or not, you are likely, at some level, still dealing with the effects and bearing the marks left behind.

Our writing experiences, along with the feedback we receive about our writing, work together to form and shape our writing identity—who we are as writers and how we see ourselves as writers. Negative experiences and harsh feedback often lead us to doubt our abilities, to think of writing as stressful and uncomfortable, and to do what we can to avoid writing altogether. Positive experiences and helpful, encouraging feedback often help us fall in love with writing and continue to enjoy it throughout our lives.

What happens when you are asked to write (or are required to write) now, as an adult? Do you jump in with confidence and energy? Or do you start to tense because you are quite sure you'll do it all wrong? Do you throw *anything* down on the page just to get it over with? Do you find yourself carrying around the weight of perfectionism? In the back of your mind, do you worry that you'll make some sort of mistake and the corrector-in-chief or grammar police will sweep in to take you out?

The truth is, if we haven't experienced a physical, daily, safe space for writing, we typically come to view writing with a suspicious side-glance. We keep writing at an arm's length, fearful that we'll be burned if we get too close.

This is not what we want for the students in our classroom. We want students to embrace writing as a vital and rich part of living a joyfully literate life instead of doing whatever they can to avoid it. In order to accomplish this, we need to look at the spaces we are providing for the students in our classroom. Are the physical layout and structure of the classroom set up in a way that helps students engage with writing? Do kids have a predictable, daily time to dig deep into writing? Have we created a safe emotional space in which writers can learn and grow?

If not, this may be why some of our students appear to be reluctant to write.

What Does This Look Like in the Classroom?

You might be thinking, "This all sounds a bit touchy-feely. What does this actually *look* like in the classroom? Are you suggesting that we all sit in a circle and give each other affirmations? Should I never correct a child when he's made a mistake in writing?"

Not exactly.

Let's explore the ways we can give kids physical space, time, and emotional space so that they can write with renewed energy and maybe even a little *joy*.

Kids Have a Central Location for All Things Writing

Some teachers utilize tables, counters, or shelves to create a writing resource area. Here, students can find anything they might need or want when it comes to writing:

- different kinds of paper
- a variety of writing utensils
- clipboards
- dry-erase boards
- envelopes
- sticky notes in various sizes
- premade blank books
- a kid-friendly picture dictionary
- lists of high-frequency words
- a class list.

Students in Ashley Dressler and Christy Karch's classroom use flexible seating during independent writing time.

If we give kids easy access to everything they need and ample choices of paper, utensils, and writing surfaces (and give them permission to go grab these items whenever they need them), it leads to autonomy and independence. Kids will feel more energized and excited to write. Bonus: Choice directly and positively impacts motivation. Since *kids* get to choose which kind of paper and utensil to use, they tend to be more motivated to dig in and write!

Kids Enjoy Flexible Seating Options

In Ashley Dressler and Christy Karch's third-grade classroom, students can choose to sit on the floor, in colorful lawn chairs, on exercise balls, on cushions near shortened tables, or in chairs at traditional tables. Flexible seating options help writers focus on the work and engage in writing because they get to *choose* (which fosters motivation) and they can settle into a place and position that is comfortable.

Kids Use Anchor Charts

Hanh-Nhi Pham's classroom walls drip with evidence of writing instruction. Clear and colorful anchor charts are displayed where students can see them as they write. These anchor charts are created in front of the students and with the students' input. Then, as kids go off to write, they can look back to the charts to help anchor them and help them remember what was taught. Once Hanh-Nhi notices that students aren't needing or accessing a chart much, she moves it off the wall to make room for new anchor charts. But she takes a picture of the anchor chart and places the picture in a three-ring binder so that kids can look at it when and if they need to.

Kids Take Risks

In Macie Harris' kindergarten classroom, students learned how to clearly state their opinions and give reasons to back those opinions up. With loads of encouragement from Macie, students learned that they could be brave, stretch themselves as writers, and jot down the sounds they heard in a word even if they were not completely confident in how to spell it. The result? Kids used rich and descriptive words in their writing rather than playing it safe by sticking to only the words they knew how to spell correctly.

Do you like restaurants? You have to try Bruno's. It has the best food ever. It should be famous! It is by the train tracks. You will love the food.

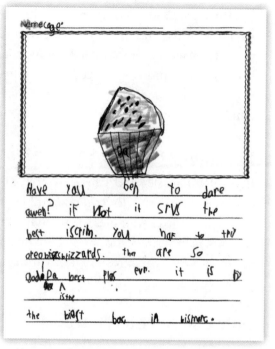

Have you been to Dairy Queen? If not, it serves the best ice cream. You have to try Oreo Blizzards. They are so good! DQ is the best place ever. It is by the biggest bank in Bismarck.

Macie worked to create a safe space where kids were celebrated for their *efforts*, not just their perfection or performance. This motivated *all* students to write because they knew that Macie wouldn't be coming down hard on them if something wasn't correct.

Kids Talk About Their Writing with a Caring and Encouraging Teacher

First-grade teacher Michelle Fitterer frequently checks in and chats with her students about their writing. Early in the year Michelle started small—just walking around talking to students casually about their writing. Over time, these chats developed into richer conversations in which Michelle could nudge a writer to try a new strategy, craft move, or convention.

Reality Check:
Standards and Rigor

In my conversations with teachers, I often hear a bit of apprehension and even a little anxiety when the topic of national, state, or local standards comes up. Many teachers feel caught between providing a physical, daily, and safe space for writing and adhering to the standards as if they are two opposing forces.

Perhaps they are not.

If we look closely at standards, we see that providing a comfortable, safe, and daily environment for writing is the bedrock on which all of the standards rest. In other words, if kids don't have the opportunity to practice and write daily, if their classroom environment is not set up in a way that fosters collaboration and independence, and if kids aren't writing in a safe emotional space, it will be almost impossible for them to reach the level of understanding and proficiency spelled out in the standards. And if we simply try to teach the bare minimum of the standards without establishing a physical, daily, and safe space for writing, our students' understanding becomes brittle and kids become apathetic and unmotivated writers.

Instead, if we make sure that all kids have a comfortable, predictable, daily time to write with a caring, encouraging adult close at hand, students improve as writers—and they may even start to *love* writing—right before our eyes!

Let's take a look at one of the foundational writing standards for writing personal narratives in second grade: CCSS.ELA-LITERACY.W.2.3. This standard asks that students "Write narratives in which they recount a well-elaborated event or short sequence of events, include details to describe actions, thoughts, and feelings, use temporal words to signal event order, and provide a sense of closure." (www.corestandards.org/ELA-Literacy/W/2/3/).

Figure 3.1 shows a writing sample from Easton, a second-grade student in Sherri Nissen's classroom.

I think we can all agree that Easton has, according to the standard, written a very strong personal narrative. Standards aside, Easton's piece is simply a delight to read! We can almost picture this child patiently waiting for what seemed like forever (in actuality, it was about thirty minutes) before the action began. As we read his piece, the scene plays out in our mind in vivid color and we might even find ourselves rooting for Easton (or the fish) as the drama plays out.

Figure 3.1

CCSS.ELA-LITERACY.W.2.3
"Write narratives in which they recount a well-elaborated event or short sequence of events, include details to describe actions, thoughts, and feelings, use temporal words to signal event order, and provide a sense of closure."

Easton has recounted an event from his life, and it's "well-elaborated." We can tell because, as we read it, we can picture what was happening when Easton landed that huge bass!

CCSS.ELA-LITERACY.W.2.3

Easton has written about what he did, what he thought, and how he felt.

CCSS.ELA-LITERACY.W.2.3

Easton has used "temporal words" and phrases to help his reader navigate the sequence of events. Instead of using formulaic (and rather boring) words like *first, next,* and *last,* he's opted for more natural words and phrases that you might use when you are telling someone a story (*one day, all of a sudden, eventually,* and *the next day*).

There's a bit of a backstory to this piece. Easton's teacher, Sherri, is a believer in the power of writing. She's also a believer in kids.

From the very first day of school until the last, students in Sherri's classroom have a large chunk of time to write. Each day, these second graders learn from published writers, watch Sherri muddle through her own writing, and then go forth and learn what it means to be a writer by . . . writing. Easton, and the other kids in his classroom, have easy access to all kinds of writing

Have you ever had a bad day fishing? I kind of did.

One day I was fishing in Wisconsin. I wasn't having very good luck. I had

been fishing for half an hour, but I didn't have one little nibble.

All of a sudden—splash! A huge bass was jumping out of the water. It was a

huge bass. I started freaking out. I grabbed the net and got it right in time. But it

wasn't over. All of a sudden, the net broke. The fish was flopping around

everywhere.

Eventually, I got it. I carried it up to my grandma and grandpa's cabin.

The next day I had it for lunch. It was tasty.

CCSS.ELA-LITERACY.W.2.3

Easton has also provided a strong "sense of closure." He has tied up all the loose ends for his reader. There's no doubt how things turned out for Easton (and the fish).

CCSS.ELA-LITERACY.W.2.3

Easton has included details about the fish's actions as well!

supplies and supports. And, each day, as the kids fan out and find comfortable places to write, Sherri floats from kid to kid, stopping to admire a student's effort, answer questions, listen, nudge, assess, and encourage.

This happens day after day.

Week after week.

Lather, rinse, repeat.

Kids in Sherri's classroom are in the habit of writing because they do it every day. And over the course of the school year, Sherri can see growth in each student. It's no surprise. Instinctively, we all know that we the more we do something, the better we get.

In Sherri's classroom, Easton is set up for success because Sherri has ensured that he has the physical space in which to write and a daily, predictable chunk of time to write.

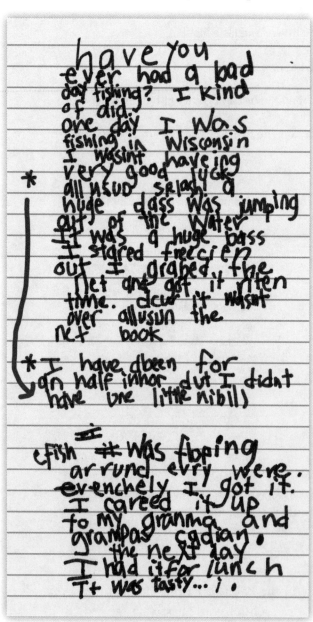

Easton's writing in his own hand.

But there's more to this story.

Sherri has also created a safe emotional space in which kids like Easton can thrive. The sample I shared with you earlier is Easton's writing, but I typed it up. The image here shows this same piece of writing in Easton's own hand.

Sherri could have responded to Easton's writing by focusing on the misspellings or lack of conventions. She could have asked him to fix everything. She could have forced him to rewrite it.

She didn't.

After admiring and complimenting Easton on all that he had done in this piece, Sherri knelt down beside him and said, *Easton, as a reader, I am confused about one thing.* She drew his attention to the fourth sentence of his piece. *What do you mean by you weren't having very good luck?* she asked.

Easton didn't hesitate. *Well, I was fishing for, like, a half an hour and I didn't even have one little nibble.*

Ah! Do you think you could add that for your reader? Sherri asked.

Easton shrugged. *I don't have any room.*

Sherri leaned in. *Let me show you what writers do when they want to add something to their writing, but they don't have any room.*

Together, Sherri and Easton added some asterisks and an arrow and Easton added the important detail to his piece.

Of course, Sherri noticed that Easton was still working on some spelling, punctuation, and capitalization skills. She would teach Easton about these things over time. But she knew that what Easton needed in order to continue to like writing and see himself as one who could write well was for her to get behind the good (or great!) work that Easton was already doing as a writer when it came to *content*.

It's pretty straightforward. If we want students to love writing and see themselves as writers, we need to be intentional about creating the spaces that allow for that to happen. Giving kids the space, time, and encouragement they need to write isn't just a nice idea. It's what enables kids to do the intense, in-depth work that writing requires.

How Can We Create a Safe and Daily Space for Writing?

So, how can we create a physical space that works *for* all writers, not *against* them? How can we make sure kids have a predictable, daily time to write? And how can we provide some safe emotional space where students can learn and grow?

Here are a handful of simple ways to create a classroom environment and schedule that allows students to engage in writing with ease. I'll also show you a few ways that you can make sure students feel emotionally safe to take some risks and thrive as writers.

Each of these ideas can help our students approach writing with confidence and maybe even a bit of enthusiasm. As you read them, reflect on your own classroom and think about how you might use them, along with some ideas of your own.

● **Arrange desks or tables in clusters to encourage conversation and collaboration.** While it's true that writers often need quiet alone time to concentrate and think deeply, most writers appreciate when this lonely endeavor is punctuated with time to talk.

If your students sit at desks, push those desks together to form small groups of three or four. If you use tables rather than desks, create a small group of students at each table. This allows kids to talk and collaborate easily. Bonus: When you stop in to chat with one writer about his writing, the other students at the table will often listen in and learn from your conversation!

You can break up the independent writing time by saying something like: Writers, *pause for a moment and share just a little bit of what you are working on right now with the partner sitting next to you,* or *Before we come together for today's minilesson, take out your writing from yesterday. Have a conversation with your partner about what you were working on yesterday and what you are going to focus on today.*

Writers can often become energized by these short, focused conversations. And hearing from other students and seeing the work they are doing helps them see what's possible in their own writing.

● **Let kids choose where they sit.** Instead of having kids sit at an assigned table or desk during writing, allow them to choose where they want to sit. Provide easy access to clipboards or dry-erase boards (anything that can serve as a hard surface) and allow students to use these as they sit or lie on the floor. These choices can be highly motivating because there is some autonomy. Plus, most of us find that we often do our best deep work when we are comfortable! No one is very productive or motivated when they are sitting in an uncomfortable position.

- **Consider playing soft music while kids write.** Some teachers have found that playing simple, soft music during writing time creates a calm and peaceful writing environment. Kerry Bishop, who teaches third grade at Lincoln Community School in Accra, Ghana, finds that the music helps kids (especially those less-than-enthused writers) transition from the lesson and settle into writing quickly. She's found that the trick is in choosing music without words; music with lyrics leads to lots of sing-alongs, but not much writing. Instead, she opts for simple and serene music like solo piano or cello. "If I'm late turning the music on, the kids will definitely remind me. They love it!" The volume should be just loud enough to serve as soothing background noise, but not loud enough to be distracting. If some kids feel more productive writing in silence, they might use headphones to help muffle the music.

- **Create a whole-group meeting area.** I've found that all students in grades K–5 benefit from a large, whole-group meeting area. Let's face it: If you are feeling anxious about writing or uninterested in writing, it's pretty tempting (and a lot more fun) to dig around in your desk for something more interesting to do during the writing lesson. So leave those desks behind and invite kids to gather in close for a short time while you are teaching the writing lesson.

There are a few things to consider when creating this whole-group space:

- **Make sure there is enough room for everyone to sit comfortably.** This is especially important to upper grades, where kids' bodies are growing! No one likes to sit in a cramped space elbow to elbow with others. So clear out a nice large space and make sure the space can fit *all* of the growing bodies in your classroom.

- **If you are having trouble finding room for such a space, rethink your teacher's desk.** Teaching isn't a desk job: perhaps you can utilize a smaller teacher's desk or simply do without. Many teachers use a countertop or shelf or small table in the corner of the room for their work space. By making your desk space smaller (or getting rid of the desk), you'll open up valuable space in the classroom that you can use to gather your students.

- **Make sure your classroom space is allocated for *learning*, not teacher storage.** Move some of those teacher boxes to a different location in the school. Or, better yet, invite a trusted colleague to help you go through your stuff and purge! This could open up some room so that you can create this space for all students to gather comfortably.

- **Repurpose existing spaces in the classroom.** If you've already created an inviting classroom library, consider using this library space as your whole-group meeting area. Personally, I think this is the perfect space to gather for writing lessons because you and your students are surrounded by the work of other writers!

- **Place an easel and chart paper in this space.** That way, you can create anchor charts or engage in modeled writing in front of your students. If you use an interactive whiteboard, make sure that all students can see it from where they sit as they gather.

- **Make writing a daily practice.** Habits are powerful. If our bodies are accustomed to exercising every day, it's easier to grab that gym bag and head to the gym. It's just something we do: we are people who exercise. If reading before bedtime is something we do each night, it becomes a habit. It becomes who we are: we are people who read at bedtime.

Our habits and choices shape who we are, what we do, and how we view ourselves. So, in order to help all students—including writers who appear to be reluctant—view themselves as people who write, make writing a daily habit in your classroom. When students expect to write each day, they are less likely to drag their feet when it's time to get started. This is especially helpful for writers who sometimes struggle to keep the writing momentum going when several days pass between writing experiences.

Carve out the time. Time is so very precious, isn't it? And here's the thing I've noticed about time: It isn't one of those things you find, like spare change under the cushions of your couch. Most teachers I know don't discover an extra forty-minute block of time in their day and wonder how to fill it. If writing is important and if we want to create space in our classroom for all writers to do good work, we need to carve out time in the day. This may require us to closely examine our practices and reevaluate how we are using these precious pearls of time in our day.

Here are some things teachers have done to carve out time for kids to write every day:

- **Reconsider the use of workbooks and worksheets.** Workbooks and worksheets claim to give students extra practice in targeted skills. It sounds good in theory, but the decontextualized exercises they provide rarely have a meaningful, sustained, positive impact on student writing. When we prioritize workbooks and worksheets over authentic writing, children begin to see writing as a complicated, rule-filled chore rather than a way to communicate and use their own voices. We can replace time spent on workbooks and worksheets with time spent on real writing.

- **Closely examine transitions throughout the day.** Transitions that are quick and smooth give us more time.

- Elicit support from a coach, a colleague, or an administrator to help you examine your daily schedule.

- **Include more turn-and-talks.** If I ask kids to raise their hands so that I can call on individual students throughout the day, it produces a sluggish feel to the lesson (and the day). It doesn't provide opportunities for everyone to participate and be heard, and it's time-consuming. Instead, invite students to share their thinking with a partner who is sitting close by. That way, you can listen in to their responses rather than take precious moments to call on each kid one at a time.

- **Start small and build slowly.** Years ago, I trained for a 5K race. I was a sprinter in high school, but I am *not* accustomed to running any kind of distance. I started small. I ran for a quarter mile and then walked the rest of the 5K. After my body became accustomed to that, I began running a half mile and walking the rest. Every week or so, I would increase my running distance by a quarter mile until, after several weeks, I was able to run the entire 5K. It took time, but I built up my stamina bit by bit.

  If you start the school year with a forty-five- to sixty-minute block of time for writing, it will likely feel overwhelming to those students who don't already love to write. Instead, consider starting out small at the beginning of the year—maybe ten to fifteen minutes of independent writing. Over time, as your students build stamina, you can increase the time.

- **Connect with kids.** In order to create a safe emotional space for kids to write, start by getting to know your kids *outside* of the writing classroom. What are they passionate about? Are they into professional soccer? Have they seen every Pixar movie ever made? Do they have brothers or sisters? Ask questions. Show genuine interest.

  Greeting kids as they arrive in the morning can also help to create an emotional space that feels safe and warm. Make eye contact. Greet them by name. Ask them about their evening. If they participate in sports or tae kwon do or music lessons outside of school, ask about these activities. Questions like, *Did your sister finally lose that tooth you were telling me about yesterday?* and *How did tae kwon do go last night?* go a long way to show kids that you care about them as individuals.

This kind of connection can help you support students during independent writing. By tapping into their interest outside of school, you can show them how real life and writing intersect. *You know how you were telling me you had to practice your free throws over and over again? You said that, over time, you noticed yourself getting better. That same perseverance is something you can bring to your writing! Just like those free throws, your writing won't be perfect the first time. But, as writers, we keep trying. And, over time, we improve!*

What I'm suggesting here goes beyond simply being *nice* or *polite* to kids. This isn't a feel-good frill. Teachers who are intentional about connecting with students and taking interest in them as *humans* find that their students are more engaged when writing.

Respect student work. We've all been there. You turn in a piece of writing and it comes back marked up with pen. At that point, you're not even given the chance to go back and fix it up. Those red pen marks (or any color of pen) create a lasting impression on us as writers. So instead of writing on students' papers, utilize a sticky note to jot down questions, thoughts, or nudges. You can place these notes in the margin of the piece or even on the back of the piece.

Writing is depth work and it requires—no, *demands*—courage. Don Graves put it this way: "Writers leave the shelter of anonymity and offer to public scrutiny their interior language, feelings and thoughts. . . . There lie both the appeal and the threat of writing. Any writer can be deeply hurt. At no point is the learner more vulnerable than in writing" (quoted in Newkirk and Kittle 2013, 22).

All students feel this vulnerability to some extent. Students who might appear reluctant often feel this acutely. And that's what can make writing seem so hard and so scary. So, tread lightly. And save the red pen for some other use.

• **Celebrate discovery and risk-taking.** I recently heard a master chef who specializes in BBQ talk about his craft. One of his remarks caught my attention. "You only learn how to make good BBQ by making bad BBQ," he proclaimed. (As a parent of a beginner trumpet player, I can attest that this is also true of learning to play the trumpet well.)

If we want to create a safe emotional space for our students, we need to embrace the fact that rich and beautiful writing, like rich and beautiful living, requires risk-taking. It requires us to try, fail, brush ourselves off, and try again—over and over again. No one is born with an ability to write perfectly right out of the gate.

So, when you see students stretching themselves by trying to spell a complex and descriptive word, celebrate the attempt, even if the word is not spelled correctly. If an emergent writer is trying a new kind of punctuation (like periods) and you notice that the child has scattered them all over (like. after. every. single. word.), instead of jumping straight to correction mode, take a moment to celebrate the fact that he was willing to trying something out.

When you celebrate discovery and risk-taking, the message you're sending is that in this classroom it's OK to try things! It doesn't *always* have to be perfect. Making approximations and attempting brave things are all part of learning to write.

Educator and writer Don Murray said, "We are coaches, encouragers, developers, creators of environments in which our students can experience the writing process for themselves" (2009, 3–4). What a noble calling we have!

Now it's your turn! What are some other ways you could establish a safe and daily time for writing in your classroom? How can you develop and create a physical space that is designed to give students every opportunity to fall in love with writing?

If you need a bit of a nudge in your thinking, here are some questions I think about when creating a safe and daily space for kids to write.

• **Is the layout of the room working for students?** One of the best ways to think about this question is to simply stand back and watch students interact with the space. Does the traffic pattern and flow work for kids when they transition from the whole-group meeting area to their spots for independent writing? Could furniture be rearranged to help? Are kids utilizing the writing resource area I've provided? If not, what could I do to make it more inviting and accessible?

- **What does my daily schedule look like?** Is the schedule realistic? If my schedule is packed and full, I'll likely feel overwhelmed and rushed—and so will my students! One of my jobs as a teacher is to take the pulse of my classroom. If it's racing, I need to slow down. Perhaps I can ask a trusted colleague, coach, or administrator to help me work through my schedule and cull the unnecessary so that I can focus on what really matters for my students.

- **How are my students feeling about writing and about themselves as writers?** If I'm not sure how my students feel, it will be more difficult for me to create a safe emotional space for them. I may want to ask my students to tell me about prior writing experiences or their feelings about writing by taking a survey or having a conversation with students.

How Can We Support a Safe Place for Writing in Our Whole-Class Work?

I hope your mind is starting to percolate with ideas for creating a space for student writers to feel energized and excited to write. Let's take a closer look at how our words and actions can help to create a safe emotional space where students can let down their guard, drop the pretense, and be seen and heard for who they are as writers.

As writers, we do quite a bit of thinking before our fingers ever touch the keys or the pen makes contact with paper. So, as teachers, it's crucial that we make this part of the writing process visible to our students so that they can see how another writer thinks.

When we think aloud and write in front of our students, we can let them see that writers take risks and sometimes experience doubt or insecurity. If *we* go first into courage, it's more likely that our students will follow. By going public with your own writing process, you send a clear message: It's OK to doubt and struggle a bit. This classroom is a safe place in which to do that.

Here are some examples of what this might sound like:

- *I'm just starting this opinion piece about wearing helmets when biking, but I am completely lost as to how to begin. I'm just going to try a bunch of beginnings aloud. If they're bad, it's OK. I think it will help me just to get some thoughts out and if one sounds like it might work, I'll try to get it down on the page.*

- *You know that, like you, I'm working on a piece about extreme weather. Already, I'm thinking I don't know a whole lot about this topic. I'm going to start by making some headings of information that might be interesting to the reader. Maybe those headings might help focus my research so that I can find out more about this topic.*

- *You know that I've been working on this piece about the time I went fishing with a friend of mine. I've got to admit: I'm a bit apprehensive about wrapping it up and then sharing it with you. In hearing this story, you—my readers—are going to find out that I'm not very good at fishing . . . yet. But I'm going to be brave because I know that part of living and part of writing is being honest and open. I want my readers to see all of me—quirks and all. Who knows—maybe it will help my reader connect with me on a different level than if I wrote about something that I do really well?*

How Can We Support a Safe Place for Writing in Our Work with Individual Students?

Creating a safe emotional space for writers can start with *you* as you think and write in front of your students. But an even more powerful way that you can create that space is by talking to individual writers. These conversations are precious and powerful because you can tailor your comments to the individual. When you coach, encourage, nudge, compliment, validate, and support individual kids, you are building a safe emotional space, one interaction at a time.

Here are some tips to help you as you work one-on-one with writers:

1. **Focus first on what the writer is doing *well*.**

   We learn primarily by building on our strengths. It's important for us to know what we are doing well so that we can continue to do it! When people notice our efforts and affirm them, it usually spurs us on to try harder and improve.

   I've heard it said that encouragement is one of the most effective of all teaching strategies. It's true. If we encourage the efforts and strengths that we see in our students—if we get behind the good work that students are doing—they'll be more likely to work hard and improve even more.

   So instead of approaching a writing conference with the mindset of "Let me see what's going on with this piece and what I need to ask them to fix," approach the conversation with curiosity and openness, looking out for all that the writer is doing *well*.

Here are a few questions to keep at the forefront of your mind when you are coaching a writer:

- What is this writer doing well?
- What are they able to do on their own?
- What are they attempting to do?

Retrain your "red-pen eyes" to look beyond the mistakes and focus on the attempts and intentions that the writer is bringing to the piece. Look for what the child is doing *well* and then tell them!

2. **Watch your language of response.**

No pressure, but I've found the words we use with writers have the power to either build a writer up or tear a writer down. This is especially true for the less-than-enthused writers in a classroom, who might already feel insecure about their writing abilities or have negative feelings about writing. We have the best of intentions, but sometimes our words can be interpreted as criticism.

So, choose your words carefully.

Here are some tips on how to talk with students in order to create a safe emotional space:

- **Start with a casual opening.** To get the conversation going, try some nonthreatening and casual openers such as these:

  - *How's it going?* This brilliant and practical opening to a conversation comes from the brilliant and practical Carl Anderson (2000).
  - *What are you working on today as a writer?*
  - *Can you show me a part of your writing that you are most proud of?*
  - *Is there a part of your writing for which I can offer support?*
  - *Is there anything I can do to help you as a writer today?*

- **Listen.** Listen to what the child is saying. *Really* listen to understand what the child is saying, instead of thinking about how you are going to respond. Once you've listened, you might follow up with, *Tell me more about that,* or *Tell me about what you were thinking when you were writing this part.* These invitations for the student to keep talking can lead to deeper thinking and conversation. When you listen intently, you are telling the child that *they matter* and they're worth your time. Those messages are powerful motivators for students who might be reluctant to write.

- **Lead with a specific compliment.** Try to avoid general and vague compliments like *Great job!* or *Nice lead!* or *I like your word choice.* I've found that the more specific the compliment, the more motivating and encouraging it can be to the writer. Be specific and let the writer know what their writing did for you *as a reader.*

  Here's what this might sound like:

  - *As a reader, when I read the first few sentences, I was hooked! I couldn't wait to read on to see what would come next.*

  - *As I read this, it feels clear and organized. My mind isn't wandering around everywhere. Your facts are put together in a way that makes sense for me as a reader.*

  - *I have to tell you, the last few sentences of your piece stuck with me. I moved on to confer with other writers, but I found myself still thinking about what you said when you ended your piece. It was powerful.*

  - *I noticed that you used several different descriptive words. These words helped to create a picture in my mind as I read!*

  - *I noticed that you started with a bit of a personal story before you jumped into the persuasive part of your piece. I think that helps your reader connect to your story.*

  - *I noticed that you're experimenting with a lot of different kinds of punctuation.*

- **Decide if you're going to teach something specific or nudge the writer to try something.** Sometimes, when you confer, you might simply listen, compliment or encourage, and then move on. Other times you might decide to nudge the writer in a particular direction or teach the writer something specific. The words you choose in these instances are important as well.

  Here are some examples of what it might sound like to nudge a writer toward revision, editing, or a new way of thinking about their writing:

  - *As a reader, I was a bit confused here. You're talking about the early life of Harriet Tubman, but then all of a sudden you're telling me about the Underground Railroad. What can you do to help your reader make that jump with you?*

  - *As a reader, I had a hard time knowing where one word ended and another word began. What can you do to help your reader?*

  - *I noticed that you used a heading in this portion of your writing, but you decided not to use one over here. Tell me more about that.*

- **End the conversation with a reminder.** Before you leave, convey your belief in the writer and remind the writer to keep doing whatever you noticed them doing well. It might sound like this:

  - *So today, I taught you that every time you are talking about yourself and using the word I, you will want to capitalize it. That's not something to remember just for this piece of writing, but for every piece that you write.*

  - *Today, I showed you one way that writers organize their writing is to use headings. Not just in this piece, but in other informational pieces that you'll write throughout your life, this is something you can include in your writing to make it clear and organized for the reader.*

3. **Be mindful of body language.**

Most of us don't do our best work or feel the most comfortable while someone is standing behind us, towering over us, and looking over our shoulder at our work. Writing is a vulnerable endeavor. Because of the nature of this tender, deep work that students are doing, I find it helpful to crouch, kneel, or squat down right next to the student. In other words, try to get as low as you can as fast as you can. Why? So that the student understands that you're here as a support—as someone who is coming alongside them to support them and their work. If kneeling is painful or difficult for you, consider using an exercise ball or rolling desk chair (set to the lowest setting) and simply roll from student to student. Since you're aiming for a posture of support, rather than opposition, avoid sitting across from the writer.

Closing Thoughts

If we want the writers in our classroom to move from passive to passionate, we need to think critically and creatively about the spaces we are providing. We, as teachers, need to take some ownership of the physical and emotional space we create for our students. When students know that they have a safe and daily space for writing, their motivation, engagement, and energy improve.

On the next page, I've listed some questions to consider as you take a reflective and honest look at your current practices in the hope of engaging all of your students—especially those students who appear to be reluctant.

If you're reading this book with a group of colleagues, use these questions to guide your shared conversation and learning.

Questions for Reflection

1. What kind of physical space have I created for my students? Is the classroom organized in a way that fosters collaboration and independence?

2. Do I have a *daily* time in my schedule that is specifically carved out for writing? If not, what can I do to make the time? Are there parts of my instructional day that I can rethink or remove?

3. Am I checking in and chatting with my students each day about their writing? If so, how is my body language and my language of response?

4. Do my students know that this is a safe place to take risks as writers and try something new, even if it might not be "correct"? If I'm not sure, how can I find out how my students are feeling about writing?

Chapter Four

Expose Writers to Real Readers

*Writing is a social act. People write
to affect the lives of others.*

—Don Graves, quoted in *Children Want to Write*

Even through the closed door, the music was deafening. My two young sons, ages four and six at the time, had navigated an iPod to their favorite song and had turned up the volume full blast.

Concerned that they would wake up the neighborhood at the early hour, I sprinted through the house toward their bedroom. Through the closed door, amid squeals and giggles, I could hear the pounding of little feet, jumping and dancing. As I reached for the door handle, I saw the note. Five words scribbled onto a sticky note and taped unceremoniously onto the door: "The Best Dancing Song Ever." (I'm conventionalizing the spelling. It actually read: "The Bst Dansing Sng Evr.")

I had to smile.

We are born with a need to be seen and heard. Don Graves noticed this in his research and work with young children. He put it this way: "Children want to write before they want to read. They are more fascinated by their own marks than by the marks of others. Young children leave their messages on refrigerators, wallpaper, moist windowpanes, sidewalks, and even on paper" (quoted in Newkirk and Kittle 2013, 23).

What happens to children's fascination with writing? Why is it that we don't see this same enthusiasm from students in many elementary school classrooms? Why do the energy and engagement fade? I think there's more going on than the mere fact that we don't allow students to do their writing on moist windowpanes. I wonder if it's because, somewhere along the way, our students have lost sight of one of the most foundational understandings about writing: writers write for *readers.*

My young sons, so enthralled with the stellar dancing song they had discovered, felt compelled to share their opinion and writing with the world—even if the world consisted only of our immediate family.

This desire to be seen and heard—to communicate with the world around them—quickly fades for most children when they enter school. At some point, writing pivots from a way to communicate and instead turns into meaningless assignments that must be completed and dropped in the teacher's basket to be graded. This kind of writing rarely goes anywhere or says anything of importance to the outside world. As a result, students begin to see writing as a chore—a mundane and sometimes miserable task that needs to be completed in order to meet the requirements of the assignment. And as a result, not surprisingly, students become less motivated and energized. Instead of a room buzzing with the excitement and energy that only true engagement can bring, many classrooms become filled with dawdling and unmotivated writers who are looking for *any* excuse *not* to write.

Reflect on Audience in Your Own Writing

So what can we do? How can we reignite our students' energy and passion for writing? I'll share some practical ideas soon, but before we explore them, I'm going to ask you to pause for a moment and reflect on your own life as a writer. I've found, in my work with students, that it helps *immensely* to consider myself first as a *writer* and then as a *teacher of writing*. When I consider the things *I* do when I write, I'm in a much better position to support kids when they engage in writing.

So, think back over the last forty-eight hours. In what types of writing have you engaged? Emails? Texts? Grocery lists? Social media posts? To-do lists? Report card comments?

Now, ask yourself: "To whom was I writing? What was the purpose?"

Chances are, you'll be able to answer both of these questions easily: You wrote the to-do list to yourself, so that you wouldn't forget to pick up the dry cleaning or a gallon of milk. The report card comments were for parents, so that they could better understand how their child is progressing.

The takeaway here is that, in life, we *almost always* write with an audience and a purpose in mind. That's what makes writing meaningful and worth the investment of our time and effort.

Mem Fox, beloved author and teacher, puts it this way: "You and I don't engage in meaningless writing exercises in real life—we're far too busy doing the real thing. And by doing the real thing we constantly learn how to do the real thing better" (1988, 114).

And yet, sadly, much of the writing that we ask students do in school falls into this "meaningless writing exercises" category that Mem Fox describes. Most of the assignments that are given to the vast majority of elementary students are devoid of a real audience or genuine purpose. As I reflect on my own beginning teaching years, I realize there were times when the audience was the teacher (me) and the purpose was a grade in my grade book. While that may have been motivating for a few of my students, it surely didn't motivate or engage the vast majority of them.

Research has found that students are more likely to become *proficient* writers who *enjoy* writing when they have some choice of topic and audience and they value the writing purpose (Graves 1994; Ball and Farr 2003; Routman 2000). In other words, it's not just a nice idea to make sure students' work reaches a real reader. This practice actually serves as a catalyst to help students improve their writing skills and enjoy the process along the way.

As writing teachers, it's our job to make sure we are providing opportunities for students to engage in writing experiences that are authentic, are connecting to an actual reader, and are worthy of their time and effort.

What Does This Look Like in the Classroom?

You might be wondering, "OK, so what does this actually *look* like in the classroom? Are you suggesting that we throw out all writing assignments and just ask kids to write emails, to-do lists, and text messages?"

Not quite.

Following are a few examples of the kinds of writing experiences that connect students to an authentic audience, invite them to write for a specific purpose, and just might increase the energy, engagement, *and* joy in the room.

Kids Take Over Some of *Your* Writing Obligations

Fifth- and sixth-grade students in Ariann Hess-Headlee's class worked in pairs to contribute short articles for the parent newsletter that was sent home. Students learned how to clearly communicate lots of information in a short text and how to collaborate with other writers. And once the parent newsletter was printed and sent home, students felt the exhilaration and joy that come from having their writing "published." Bonus: Parents were more likely to actually *read* the newsletter because the kids were excited to show them the article that they contributed!

Kids Offer Help to Community Organizations

After reading and studying a myriad of travel brochures, second-language learners in Kathy Haskins' fourth-grade North Dakota classroom worked with a partner to create their own brochures. The brochures, which showcased family-friendly activities

5th Grade Newsletter

VOLUME NO. 1   Friday, May 10, 2019   ISSUE# 30

Math
By: Shayne Black & Bridger Hughes

This week in math we worked on making estimations in word problems and figuring out the exact answers. After we finished figuring out both we compared them! We did some as a class and then for our assignment. We had to annotate the problem to help us figure out the important words, numbers and underline the question. Estimating was super fun! We had a great time and we can't wait to see what we are working in next!

Science
By Riley and Jory

Shadow Activity

Part of our science this week was the shadow activity. For this activity we went outside to trace our feet, and every hour after that we traced our shadows and measured them. We also documented the direction the sun was and the direction of the shadow. After that, we took the information we had collected and created graph. We glued them in our notebooks

and then wrote a summary about what we did. We had fun!

Star Posters

The rest of science this week was spent researching stars. We wrote down what we learned while researching,then Mrs. Hess-Headlee separated us into groups of four. The groups began by creating a rough draft of what our poster was going to look like. Then as a group we combined the

1

Students contributed short articles for the parent newsletter.

in their town, were polished and photocopied and then given to the local chamber of commerce to display. The brochures were also given to families who were new to the area.

All writers jumped in with a fresh enthusiasm because they knew that the writing wasn't simply going to be dropped in the teacher's basket for a grade. The final piece would be shared with actual readers!

SPLASH DOWN

Are you ready to get soaking wet? Go to Splash Down at the Dakota Square Mall (2400 10th St. SW). You can have a birthday party there, slide down the many water slides, or play video games. Take your family to Splash Down and have a great time. It's located in the Mall.

DAKOTA SQUARE MALL

How would you like to have fun for the whole family? You can eat different kind of food, watch a movie, shop for clothes, take a break with the dinosaurs and rides, splash down in the water slides and play games. How about taking a break, drink coffee and read your favorite book. Its open from 10 am to 9 pm. Please come to the mall and have fun shopping in the 98 stores.

MAYSA ARENA

DO YOU WANT TO LEARN HOW TO ICE SKATE OR PLAY HOCKEY? YOU CAN! COME AND HAVE A GREAT TIME SKATING, TAKING LESSONS, JUST SKATE FOR FUN, OR ENJOY YOUR BIRTHDAY PARTY THERE. YOU CAN ALSO WATCH OUR FAMOUS MINOTAURO PLAY HOCKEY. WHERE DO YOU GET TO WATCH ALL THIS ACTION? COME TO 2501 W. BURDICK EXPY. SO BRING THE FAMILY AND BUNDLE UP FOR GREAT DAY OF ICE EVENTS.

DISCOVER

THE MAGIC CITY OF MINOT

WINTER FUN ACTIVITIES

HENRY MINOT

THE TOWN WAS NAMED AFTER HENRY DAVIS MINOT WHO WAS A RAILROAD INVESTOR AND AN ORNITHOLOGIST. THE TOWN WAS INCORPORATED ON JUNE 28, 1887.

IT IS KNOWN AS THE MAGIC CITY BECAUSE OF THE GREAT NORTHERN RAILROAD. WHEN THE CREW CAME TO THE LAND, THE CITY MAGICALLY APPEARED OVERNIGHT.

Students worked together in partners to create brochures featuring family-friendly activities in town.

DAKOTA TERRITORY AIR MUSEUM

Are you ready to go back in History? Go to the Dakota Territory Air Museum and see planes from everywhere! To find us, go to 100 34th Ave. NW. You can have a membership, bring your child for classes, have an event or birthday party, and even climb into the airplanes. So take your family and experience the fun of being a pilot.

Magic City Discovery Science Center

Want to know where bad lights go? To prism. Just kidding. Really, do you want to learn how to operate a crane, fly scarves through wind tunnels, and build your own race track? Well come to the Magic City Discovery Science Center located in the Dakota Territory Air Museum. What a great place for children of all ages to discover science using your hands. You want get there early because it is only open from November to March. So take your family to be scientists and explode our world.

ROOSEVELT PARK ZOO

READY TO EXPERIENCE YOUR WILD SIDE? GO TO ROOSEVELT PARK ZOO. YOU WILL SEE THE MOST EXOTIC ANIMALS FROM AROUND THE WORLD. COME SEE THE JAPANESE SEROW, AN OKAPI, RED PANDAS, AND MORE. THEY EVEN OFFER FUN FILLED CAMPS FOR CHILDREN OF ALL AGES AND THEY HAVE ADULT EVENTS TOO, A BEAUTIFUL GIFT SHOP, FOOD, AND YOU CAN EVEN HAVE EVENTS THEIR FOR YOUR FAMILY. MEMBERSHIPS ARE AVAILABLE, BUT WITH THAT YOU CAN GET INTO OTHER ZOOS ACROSS THE USA WITH THAT MEMBERSHIP. COME TO BOO AT THE ZOO AND CHRISTMAS AT THE ZOO WITH YOUR FAMILY. SO WHY NOT COME AND SEE WHAT THE ZOO HAS TO OFFER. JUST GO TO 1219 BURDICK EXPRESSWAY EAST.

North Hill Bowl

Can you knock down pins? Go to North Hill bowl with the family. There are leagues for seniors, youth, men, and women. They also have extreme bowling on Friday and Saturday evenings from 6pm-1am using black lights. Shoe rentals are available and bumper pads for the little ones. Go to 1901 North Broadway and strike a lively family evening of bowling.

PLANET PIZZA

Experience an out of this world family center with great food and awesome games. It's open from 11am to 9pm. The main food is pizza, but they also have space sandwiches, breadsticks, pasta, and space baskets. First, it is a family center because parents can sit and chat while the kids are playing video games. There are over 30 video games. Next, try the bouncy houses for the younger children and for older ones. Final, play a game of laser tag. Go to 220 S. Broadway and bounce your way to Planet Pizza and amuse the whole family.

Kids Get Involved in a Real Issue Under Discussion

Renae Ely's third-grade students at Liberty Elementary in Bismarck, North Dakota, had the opportunity to design an all-inclusive playground for their school. In addition to learning about area and perimeter, force and motion, and engineering and designing 3D models, the students learned how to craft powerful persuasive pieces to go along with their ideas. The designs, along with the writing pieces, were presented to the local parks and recreation committee for consideration. Bonus: Students were highly motivated to do the hard work of revision and editing because they knew their writing pieces were going to be seen by community leaders.

Kids Decide Who Needs to Hear Their Message

After working with Melissa Potts' first-grade students as they created their own how-to posters, I gathered the students to talk about the work we had done and to reflect on what we had learned. I asked students to think about where they might display their posters. I told them that I was planning on putting my how-to poster about laundry up in my laundry room at home as a way to help my two sons, who were learning how to do their own laundry.

Who might benefit from reading your work? I asked.

As the students turned to share their ideas with a partner, I noticed a dramatic shift in the energy and excitement in the room.

- *I could put my poster in the library since it's about how to find a good book!*

- *I'm going to put mine right next to our cubbies! My poster teaches people how to get their snow pants, coats, and boots on before recess!*

- *Mine's on how to play kickball. Maybe Mrs. Christiansen would let me put it up outside!*

What struck me was that simply suggesting that their writing could *go* somewhere and *accomplish* something created an entirely new and almost electric energy in the room.

As I left the room, I heard one of the students ask his teacher if he and his classmates could keep working on their posters. The teacher obliged and, after a collective cheer (yes, *cheer!*) from the students, they continued writing. As I looked around the classroom, I couldn't find one unmotivated, disengaged, or distracted student in the entire room.

The bathroom passes hung quietly near the door.

I would have counted that as success, but this story has a little something extra: When I arrived at the school the next morning, Melissa called me into her classroom. She explained that one student, Brock, had been so inspired and excited by the previous day's writing experience that when he got home, he asked his mom to help him make homemade play dough. Brock then hopped on his family's laptop computer and created *another* instructional poster to teach his friends how to make their own. The teacher showed me Brock's new poster, along with the individual bags of homemade play dough that he'd brought in to give to each of his classmates.

Friends, writing is a social endeavor. It was always meant to be a means by which we could be seen and heard—to communicate with the world around us. However, if students are simply completing assignments and turning them in for a grade, is it any wonder why we see the shrug, the slump, and the sharpening

Brock created another instructional poster to teach his friends how to make homemade play dough.

of pencils when we ask students to write? Without an actual audience to read and respond and react to our writing, the hard work just isn't worth it.

Instead, if we invite students to do the real work of writing—if we invite them to write for readers who matter to them—we just might find the key that unlocks true engagement and energy.

Reality Check:
Standards and Rigor

Many of us work in schools where our teaching (and student learning) must be closely aligned to local, state, or national standards. Rest assured, the kind of writing I'm proposing—writing that reaches out to an authentic audience, writing that is meaningful, purposeful, and maybe even *fun—can and does* align to standards. It's rigorous and deep work to create something that will leave the classroom and be read by others. It just also happens to be very engaging and motivating.

Let's take a look at the instructional poster in Figure 4.1 that Brock created in class (before he went home and created one about how to make homemade play dough) and see how this engaging and authentic experience stacks up next to the Common Core writing standards that are required in the state of Montana, where Brock attends school (Montana Office of Public Instruction 2011).

Figure 4.1

CCSS-ELA-LITERACY.W.1.2
"Write informative/explanatory texts in which they name a topic, supply some facts about the topic, and provide some sense of closure."

Brock has clearly named his topic ("How to Play Kickball") and named several facts about kickball in the form of numbered steps and things you need (like "strong legs" and "fast running"). He has also provided a sense of closure ("Now you know how to play kickball!").

CCSS-ELA-LITERACY.W.1.7
"Participate in shared research and writing projects (e.g., explore a number of 'how-to' books on a given topic and use them to write a sequence of instructions)."

Before students created their own instructional posters, we worked together to examine a number of instructional posters. These posters served as mentor texts that were used by students to help them create their own.

(CCSS-ELA-LITERACY.W.1.5
"With guidance and support from adults, focus on a topic, respond to questions and suggestions from peers, and add details to strengthen the writing as needed."

Before he began writing, Brock and his classmates had the opportunity to tell a partner about their topic and the kinds of information they would include in their poster. This allowed each student, including Brock, to "respond to questions and suggestions from peers." As the teacher and I conferred with individual writers, we were able to coach them in how to "add details to strengthen [the] writing."

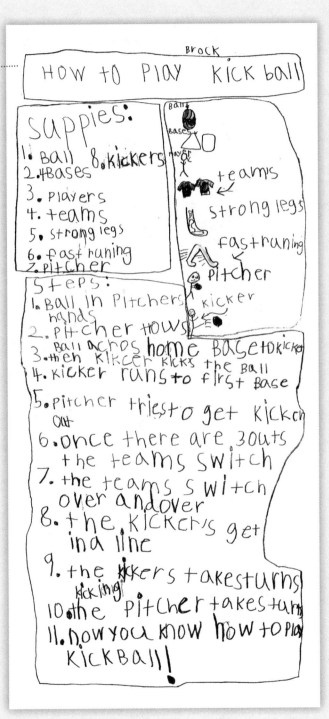

CCSS.ELA-LITERACY.L.1.2
"Demonstrate command of the conventions of standard English capitalization, punctuation, and spelling when writing."

CCSS.ELA-LITERACY.L.1.2.B
"Use end punctuation for sentences."

CCSS.ELA-LITERACY.L.1.2.D
"Use conventional spelling for words with common spelling patterns and for frequently occurring irregular words."

(CCSS.ELA-LITERACY.L.1.2.E
"Spell untaught words phonetically, drawing on phonemic awareness and spelling conventions."

While crafting his instructional poster, Brock has attended to capitalization, punctuation, and spelling. Bonus: He has paid close attention to these things not because he's been worried about his grade on the assignment, but rather because it has mattered to him that his ideas are clearly communicated!

CCSS-ELA-LITERACY.W.1.8
"With guidance and support from adults, recall information from experiences or gather information from provided sources to answer a question."

Brock has thought back on what he knows about kickball and has recalled "information from experiences" while creating his poster about how to play kickball.

How do the travel brochures from Kathy Haskins's fourth-grade students stack up when we compare them to the Common Core State Standards? Figure 4.2 identifies how the brochure meets a range of writing standards.

The brochures also gave Kathy an opportunity to teach multiple conventions, all of which align with the standards:

- "Produce complete sentences, recognizing and correcting inappropriate fragments and run-ons." (L.4.1j)
- "Produce complex and compound-complex sentences." (L.4.1k)
- "Use possessive nouns." (L.4.1l)
- "Form and use the progressive (e.g., *I was walking; I am walking; I will be walking*) verb tenses." (L.4.1m)
- "Form and use the perfect (e.g., I had walked; I have walked; I will walk) verb tenses." (L.4.1n)
- "Resolve issues of complex and contested usage, consulting reliable references as needed." (L.4.1p)

Figure 4.2

CCSS.ELA-LITERACY.W.4.4
"Produce clear and coherent writing in which the development and organization are appropriate to task, purpose, and audience."

The brochure is clear and coherent. It's organized in a way to be appealing and clear to the reader and it accomplishes the purpose of telling the reader about the various points of interest in Minot.

CCSS.ELA-LITERACY.W.4.5
"With guidance and support from peers and adults, develop and strengthen writing as needed by planning, revising, and editing."

In creating the brochure, the students planned, revised, and edited as needed. The result is a clear and visually appealing piece.

CCSS.ELA-LITERACY.W.4.6
"Use technology, including the Internet, to produce and publish grade-level writing using keyboarding skills/digital tools as well as to interact and collaborate with others."

With support from other writers and the teacher, the students used technology to find specific information to include in each section. Although each student worked on a section individually, all students collaborated and used digital tools to complete the finished product.

CCSS.ELA-LITERACY.W.4.7
"Conduct short research projects that build knowledge through investigation of different aspects of a topic."

Creating a brochure doesn't require a long period of time. Instead, this was a short project that encouraged students to grow and build their knowledge through investigation.

CCSS.ELA-LITERACY.W.4.8
"Recall relevant information from experiences or gather relevant information from print and digital sources; take notes and categorize information, and provide a list of sources."

Many of the students who worked to create this brochure have been to the places they highlighted in their writing. In that way, they recalled the relevant information from their experiences. If they felt that they needed to add more information, they gathered that information from print and digital sources.

CCSS.ELA-LITERACY.W.4.2b
"Develop the topic with facts, definitions, concrete details, quotations, or other information and examples related to the topic."

The writer has clearly developed the topic and included specific details about the water park, such as where it is located and the kinds of things you can do there.

CCSS.ELA-LITERACY.W.4.2a
"Introduce a topic clearly and group related information in paragraphs and sections; include formatting (e.g., headings), illustrations, and multimedia when useful to aiding comprehension."

Throughout this brochure, the writers have made their topic clear to the reader. They have also grouped information into sections and used pictures to keep the piece clear and organized.

SPLASH DOWN

Are you ready to get soaking wet? Go to Splash Down at the Dakota Square Mall (2400 10th St. SW). You can have a birthday party there, slide down the many water slides, or play video games. Take your family to Splash Down and have a great time. It's located in the Mall.

DAKOTA SQUARE MALL

How would you like to have fun for the whole family? You can eat different kind of food, watch a movie, shop for clothes, take a break with the dinosaurs and rides, splash down in the water slides and play games. How about taking a break, drink coffee and read your favorite book. Its open from 10 am to 9 pm. Please come to the mall and have fun shopping in the 98 stores.

MAYSA ARENA

DO YOU WANT TO LEARN HOW TO ICE SKATE OR PLAY HOCKEY? YOU CAN! COME AND HAVE A GREAT TIME SKATING, TAKING LESSONS, JUST SKATE FOR FUN, OR ENJOY YOUR BIRTHDAY PARTY THERE. YOU CAN ALSO WATCH OUR FAMOUS MINOTAURO PLAY HOCKEY. WHERE DO YOU GET TO WATCH ALL THIS ACTION? COME TO 2501 W. BURDICK EXPY. SO BRING THE FAMILY AND BUNDLE UP FOR GREAT DAY OF ICE EVENTS.

High Air Ground

Are you ready to jump to the sky? Drive to Oak Park Village on 4th Ave. NW. Come enjoy the surf boards, trampoline parks, baby pits, and dodgeball. They even have toddler time for the little ones. So take your family to Jump for fun at High Air Ground from 10:00am to 8:00pm.

DISCOVER
THE MAGIC CITY OF MINOT

WINTER FUN ACTIVITIES

HENRY MINOT

THE TOWN WAS NAMED AFTER HENRY DAVIS MINOT WHO WAS A RAILROAD INVESTOR AND AN ORNITHOLOGIST. THE TOWN WAS INCORPORATED ON JUNE 28, 1887.

IT IS KNOWN AS THE MAGIC CITY BECAUSE OF THE GREAT NORTHERN RAILROAD. WHEN THE CREW CAME TO THE LAND, THE CITY MAGICALLY APPEARED OVERNIGHT.

CCSS.ELA-LITERACY.W.4.2e
"Provide a concluding statement or section related to the information or explanation presented."

In each section of the brochure, the writers have provided a final sentence that wraps up that section and provides a sense of closure for the reader.

CCSS.ELA-LITERACY.W.4.2d
"Use precise language and domain-specific vocabulary to inform about or explain the topic."

The writer has provided clear and precise language about how the city got its name (and nickname). The information that the writer has provided helps to inform the reader and explain more about the topic.

It's clear, isn't it? Writing experiences like these aren't just engaging activities that increase motivation and help even those less-than-enthused writers to *enjoy* writing. They are rich opportunities for students to wrestle with the complexities of writing that are represented in state and local standards. Students are willing and even excited to dive into these types of writing experiences largely because they want their ideas to be communicated clearly to a reader who matters.

How Can We Give Students Opportunities to Connect to Readers Who Matter to Them?

So how do we connect our students to readers who matter to them? How can we harness this powerful tool and invite all students to engage in the deep and thoughtful work of writing?

I've listed several simple ways to connect student writers to authentic readers here. Each of these ideas can help less-than-enthusiastic writers (and all writers) approach writing with a renewed energy and passion. My hope is that these ideas will serve as a spark to ignite some ideas of your own!

- **Invite students to write book reviews.** Instead of requiring students to write a summary or short response after they finish a book, show them what real readers do! After reading several book reviews together as a class (Goodreads or Amazon book reviews are great places to start), show them how to create their own! Many teachers type them up and tape them to the inside back cover of books in the classroom library. Or the reviews can be placed on the shelves of the school or public library, much like the ones you would see at retail bookstores. Students are motivated to do the hard the hard work of revision and editing because they know their writing is going to be displayed for everyone to see!

- **Host a publishing party.** Once students have completed a piece of writing, invite them to celebrate their hard work by throwing a simple but fun publishing party. Play some jaunty music, serve healthy snacks and beverages, and give students time to admire the work of other writers. Have students place their finished piece on their desk or table, alongside a blank piece of paper and a pencil. Then, invite students to visit other students' desks, read the piece of writing, and leave a compliment on the blank sheet of paper. The beauty of this kind of publishing party is that all students are reading and writing during the entire experience! And students love to read the compliments left by their classmates.

- **Host a virtual authors party.** Consider posting student work on a blog or classroom website for parents and other community members to enjoy anytime. In addition to the finished pieces, many teachers include photographs showing students engaging in the writing process. Knowing that their writing will be published online can be extremely motivating.

- **Provide daily time for writers to share their work.** Each day, at the conclusion of writing time, carve out three or four minutes and give students the opportunity to share their writing work from that day with a partner. This simple yet powerful experience allows students to "publish" their writing right away, even if it's still in draft form.

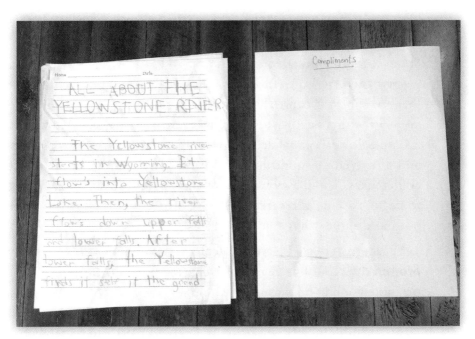

Students read other students' work and then leave a compliment for each writer.

For students learning English as an additional language, it also provides an opportunity to practice using and hearing English in a low-stakes setting (with a partner rather than the entire class). These informal opportunities for students to share their work also allow students to see how another writer is approaching the task, giving them a little nudge to try something new in their own writing.

- **Partner with student writers to co-author your sub plans.** No, I'm not talking about the *instructional* parts of your sub plans. I'm talking about the daily procedures and routines such as attendance protocol, morning routines, bathroom or hall pass procedures, lunch room or recess dismissal, and so on. Invite partners or small groups to work together to write simple and clear step-by-step directions so that any guest teacher will be able to keep things running smoothly in your absence. You can bind these authentic procedural texts into a book and share it with substitute teachers. If you make multiple copies of the book, you can also give them to new students who join your classroom later in the school year. Most kids are more than a little motivated by a writing experience like this because *they* are the ones who are annoyed when a guest teacher visits the classroom and doesn't know the routines!

- **Show students how to create their own PSAs.** After students have viewed and listened to several public service announcements, invite them to choose a cause that is important to them and then work alone or with a partner to create their own PSA, using iMovie or a simple PowerPoint slide. One school utilized a projection system and displayed the students' PSAs in the foyer during parent-teacher conferences. While they waited for their parent-teacher conference to begin, parents and caregivers were able to view the PSAs and find out more about what students were learning.

- **Let students create informative or persuasive posters to display around the school.** Instead of purchasing premade posters to promote good hand-washing techniques, show how to cover your cough, or provide other school health reminders, ask students to create them! Students will be more likely to read and remember the information when the posters are student-created, and the creator of the poster will feel empowered knowing that they are contributing something important to the school community.

- **Create "rule reminders" posters to prevent playground problems.** I recently worked with a fifth-grade teacher who was noticing that students were experiencing an increase of frustration, anger, and fights over tetherball at recess. The students were arguing over the rules of the game. Why not use this as an opportunity to engage in informational and procedural writing? Students could read and research to find out what the official rules are and then create a bright and engaging poster (along with photographs) to help keep things consistent and fair on the playground.

- **Show students how writing can help solve classroom challenges.** One student recently approached his teacher to express his frustration over how turn-and-talks were going when there was a group of three rather than the typical partner structure. His teacher helped him to think of ways to solve the challenge and encouraged him to use writing to help navigate interaction with a group of three. The student created a clear and informative reminder to share with his group. Problem solved!

- **Give the gift of writing.** For narrative writing, encourage students to think of a person who would appreciate receiving this piece of writing as a gift. For example, if I'm writing about the time my older sister taught me how to ride a bike without training wheels, perhaps I could give *her* the final piece. As students write, encourage them to think of the person to whom they will give the writing and let that influence the words, tone, and angle they choose for their writing. When the writing is finished, provide special ribbons and small notecards to include with the writing. Knowing that the writing will be given to a particular person helps to keep engagement high throughout the writing process.

- **Reconsider the writing assignments you already give students.** How might you tweak them so that the writing reaches an authentic audience? A research report on a state might become a travel brochure to be duplicated and distributed. A how-to piece might become a poster that focuses on something genuinely useful to kids in your school—navigating the school cafeteria or joining a game at recess—and gets displayed in a useful location in the school.

Your turn! What kinds of writing tasks are you currently asking your students to complete? How could you tweak them so that students are still engaging in that type of writing but are writing to an authentic audience?

If you're feeling stuck, here's a list of questions I consider when creating writing experiences that cause kids to think beyond the four walls of the classroom and reach to the world outside.

- **What genre am I asking students to write in?** Is the writing going to be factual and informative? Am I asking them to give an opinion or try to persuade? Are they putting forth a narrative from their own lives?

- **In the real world, where do we see this type of writing?** For example, if I'm asking students to create procedural writing, I'll want to think about where I see this kind of writing in the world outside of school. In terms of procedural writing, I don't see a whole lot of pieces of paper floating around with numbered steps showing how to make a peanut-butter-and-jelly sandwich. But I do see procedural writing *everywhere*: in the TSA line at the airport, at the gas pump, and at my dentist's office, just to name a few.

- **Is there a need for this kind of writing in my school or community?** Start small! If the thought of sharing student writing with places in my town or city sounds overwhelming, I think about the kinds of procedural writing that could be published around the school. Is the PE teacher complaining about kids walking on the gym floor with their snow boots on? Are kids frustrated with how slow the hot lunch line is going? Perhaps students can create pieces of writing to help solve these problems and make things run more smoothly.

  Here, I'll add a caveat: I have seen well-meaning teachers invent scenarios and needs that did not really exist in the interest of giving students a sense of purpose. Yet, consider what happens in that moment when the children find that no wealthy philanthropist is, after all, considering where to build a zoo, and that their impassioned letters about why their community would be an ideal place for such a zoo will not be read by anyone other than their teacher. A teacher who had lived through this experience told me that, in the moments that followed her confession, a stunned silence fell over the classroom. Then came the anger, hot and swift. The students knew they had been tricked. I understand that sometimes we, as teachers, are desperate to try anything to motivate our students to write, but we don't need to resort to manipulation or flat-out dishonesty. There is always another way.

Here's an example of how these three questions helped guide first-grade teachers at Liberty Elementary in Bismarck, North Dakota, as they considered ways to connect their writers with readers. As part of the mandated curriculum, students were expected to research and write an informational piece about an endangered animal.

The teachers could have simply taught the kids how to write an endangered animal report, but instead, they considered each question this way:

- **What genre am I asking students to write in?** The teachers planned to ask the students to engage in informational writing, in order to meet the requirements of a particular standard. Even more specifically, they planned to ask students to write about an endangered animal, to align with their curriculum.

- **In the real world, where do we see this type of writing?** The teachers immediately thought about the Dakota Zoo in Bismarck. Near the entrance to the zoo there is a building called the Discovery Center—a big barn that houses the aquariums, hands-on materials for children and visitors, as well as educational posters and displays about the animals.

- **Is there a need for this kind of writing in my school or community?** The teachers wondered if students could create their own informational posters about an endangered animal and then display the posters in the Discovery Center. They contacted the zoo and, not surprisingly, the staff was thrilled to partner with the teachers and students in this project.

Student-created informational poster

Students engaged in shared research, drafting, and revising as they created their posters. Then they created QR codes with voice threads to explain their learning with visitors at the zoo. Once the students' posters and QR codes were displayed, anyone with a QR reader on their mobile device could scan the codes and listen to the first graders share their learning and their writing. To top off the experience, the teachers and students took a field trip to the zoo to see their work on display! The students were engaged and excited throughout the entire process because they knew that their writing was going to be shared with the visitors at the zoo.

How Can We Leverage the Power of an Authentic Audience?

I'm hoping that your mind is now percolating with ideas of how you can connect your writers to actual readers. The possibilities are limited only by your imagination, so dream big!

Once you've created experiences that connect student writers to readers, you are poised to consider another question: How can you effectively leverage the enormous power that this can have on your less-than-enthusiastic writers?

Here are a few suggestions:

1. **Start with real-world models.**

   As writers, we lean on other writers to see what is possible in our own writing. For example, I'm guessing that, before writing our first résumé, many of us looked closely at the résumés of others. Proficient writers are careful and observant readers, noticing what other authors do and then using what they've seen to make their own writing stronger. Simply put, it helps to see what a finished product looks like—to see what we are aiming for.

The same is true for the kids in our classroom. So, if you ask students to create instructional posters, gather a few examples from the real world. Bring in a poster from the dentist's office (how to floss your teeth), the DMV (how to gather the paperwork needed to renew your license), or the school bathroom (how to wash your hands). If students will be creating brochures, bring in samples of brochures that are available in hotels, airports, and travel agencies. (Bonus: These are *free!*) It can be extremely motivating to see what a fancy, finished, published poster or brochure looks like.

2. **Think aloud and demonstrate your own thinking before you write.**

Early on in my teaching career, my mentor told me, "One of the most effective teaching moves you can make is to crack open your thinking and let your students see and hear what's going on in your mind as you write." That's good advice. We can't simply *tell* kids to keep the reader in mind as they write. We need to *show* them how we do this and how it keeps us focused and motivated right out of the gate.

To see what this looks like in practice, let's take a peek at a lesson that Anna Jaross taught.

Anna is a second-grade teacher in Sammamish, Washington. Anna was beginning a writing unit focused on persuasive writing. Instead of asking all of her students to write a letter to the principal asking for an extra recess or to the cafeteria staff asking for more chocolate milk, Anna decided to show her students how to choose topics and readers that mattered to *them*.

Before Anna asked her students to engage in this work, she showed students how *she* chose a topic and an authentic audience for her writing.

With her students gathered to watch, Anna began thinking aloud about her life and the topics and issues that were currently in her heart and mind. She and her family had recently added a puppy named Wilson to their family. She shared that, as a pet owner, one of her new responsibilities was to walk Wilson each day and pick up after him. She told her students that, although she loved the colorful bags she had purchased from the company Bags on Board, she had noticed that they were not compostable. This wasn't an idea she had read about it in some teacher's manual. It was something that was honestly bothering her.

Anna shared that one day, while walking Wilson, she realized that she was throwing away two to three bags a day and that these bags would be sitting in a landfill for a very long time. Right then and there she decided to write a letter to the company that made the bags in the hope of persuading them to begin making the bags out of biodegradable materials. As she shared all of this, her second graders sat wide-eyed and tuned in to her every word.

Before Anna even began writing, she was showing students that writers think about their readers *from the very start*. This sets the stage for engagement and investment. Anna was sending the message that, as a writer, she was first and foremost thinking about where this writing might go and who might read it.

Now that Anna had demonstrated this important facet of writing, she could invite her students to consider topics and issues from their own lives and then guide them as they chose an audience who mattered to them. All of the writers in her classroom were drawn in because they knew that *they* were in the driver's seat in terms of topic and audience. And it was exciting to imagine how their writing might be published and shared beyond the classroom.

3. **Show students how *you* consider your reader as you write.**

Anna continued to crack open her thinking as she began crafting her persuasive letter. *I want to make sure my request is clear,* she explained, *but I also want to make sure I'm really respectful in the way I ask the company to change the way they are making these bags. I think the company will be more willing to consider my idea if I come across as kind and respectful. Let me try a few sentences aloud and think about how they might sound to the person at the company who might read my letter.*

As writers, you and I are constantly considering our audience throughout the writing process. We subconsciously make choices and adjustments as we write so that we can clearly and effectively communicate with the person or people to whom we are writing. Considering the reader helps us stay engaged and helps improve our writing.

While you may not write your entire piece in front of students, I find it helpful to write at least a portion of it in front of the kids. That way, you can crack open your thinking again and let your students see that, as we write, we're constantly asking ourselves questions such as these:

- Will this make sense to the reader?

- Am I using words that the reader will understand?

- Will this engage the reader?

- Am I giving too much information? Not enough?

- Does this reader need the facts only? Or do I need to add something that will connect with the reader on an emotional level?

- Have I struck the right tone? Should my tone be formal or more informal and conversational?

Let your students see (and hear) you wrestle with questions like these. In doing so, you are showing your students how you keep the reader at the forefront of your mind.

Date 3-15

Dear Bags on Board.

Greetings! I am a dog owner in Sammamish, WA. As every dog owner knows, a good, sturdy doggy poop bag is a must. I was happy using your brand of doggy poop bags. They are a good price and do the job.

However, there is a problem. Bags on Board doggy poop bags are 100% plastic and are not compostable. I believe Bags on Board should change to a compostable bag.

Yes, I was lured in by the pretty rainbow of colors, but these colorful bags will sit in landfills for hundreds of years! Plastic bags are also polluting our lakes, rivers and oceans. Sealife is dying because of this!

Please consider changing your doggy poop bags to compostable. It will help out environment for generations to come.

Sincerely

Anna

Teacher Anna Jaross modeled how she wrote a letter to a company that makes bags for dog waste.

When we think aloud and model how we consider our audience throughout the writing process, we send a clear message to our students: writers write for readers. And writing for readers is a lot more motivating than writing for the teacher!

4. **Coach individual writers.**

Even if you've done an over-the-top stellar job of sharing real-world models and thinking aloud about how to keep your reader in mind, students will still need your support once they begin the hard work of writing on their own.

Here are some tips to help you as you coach writers:

- **Show genuine interest.** Before the work is published and shared beyond your classroom, it will likely be shared with *you*. You are the first (and most important) reader, so make sure you are sending this message loud and clear: *You are important. Your writing is important. I value you and your writing.* Smile. Look the student in the eye. Laugh heartily at the funny parts. Sigh or hold your hand to your heart at the touching parts. As a writer

myself, there is nothing more motivating than knowing that my words are having an impact on my reader. Help your students to know that their writing is having an impact on *you*.

- **Ask questions.** Not only does asking questions show that you're interested in the student (and his writing), but well-placed questions can often redirect students whose engagement has started to fade. Here are some questions to spur thinking and help students reengage: *To whom are you writing? Who are you hoping will read your work? What do you know about your reader? Is this reader younger than you or older than you? How is that helping you choose the kinds of words to include in your writing? Reread what you've just written, but pretend that you're the reader. Does it sound OK? Does it make sense?*

- **Use the phrase "as a reader."** Many well-meaning teachers go into a kind of teacher mode when they coach a writer. Instead, try to think of yourself as a *reader*. As you listen to a child share their writing, consider what is going on in your mind as a reader and then tell the student about it. For example, you could say something like: *This part of your writing helped me, as a reader, to create a movie in my head. I could actually picture exactly what you were describing!* Or *The first few sentences of your piece hooked me, as a reader, right away and made me want to keep reading!* If you need to nudge the writer, you could say: *As a reader, I was confused when I read this paragraph. What could you do to help your reader?* By using the phrase "as a reader," you're reminding the student that the ultimate goal is to connect with the reader. This helps writers keep their eyes on the goal.

Closing Thoughts

We don't want to waste our time (or our students' time) simply creating "meaningless writing exercises." We want our classroom and the students in that classroom to come alive with energy, enthusiasm, and passion each time they write.

If we want our writers to be invested and engaged and immersed in writing, then we need to think beyond the four walls of our classroom and help our students reach the world (and readers) beyond.

Following are a few questions to consider as you take a reflective and honest look at your current practices in the hope of engaging all your students—especially students who might appear to be reluctant.

If you're reading this book with a group of colleagues, use these questions to guide your shared conversation and learning.

Questions for Reflection

1. Am I providing students an opportunity to share their writing work with a partner each day?

2. When I write in front of my students, am I modeling how considering my audience influences how I write and what I write?

3. Am I providing opportunities for students to share their writing with the outside world?

4. Are there multiple opportunities in my classroom to share and celebrate students' writing?

Chapter Five

Offer Choice

Motivation and energy hinge on choices.

—Donna Skolnick, educator and author

Ours is a culture that values choice.

I was pondering this a while back as I waited in line to order my coffee (a sixteen-ounce sugar-free vanilla latte with almond milk, extra hot, no foam, if you must know). As I eavesdropped on the customers in line in front of me, I couldn't help but marvel at the myriad of choices we make when ordering something as simple as coffee. As adults, we make countless choices every day. These choices make life rich, full, and interesting.

When my children were younger, a good friend of mine gave me some valuable advice. "Whenever possible," she said, "give your kids choices. 'Would you like peas or carrots with your dinner?' 'Would you like to brush your teeth now or in five minutes?' 'Would you like to wear your coat or carry your coat?'"

My friend explained that, in providing choices, I would be giving my children voice, ownership, and even a little power in their own lives while still making sure they ate their vegetables, brushed their teeth, and had a coat with them in cold weather.

When we are given choices instead of being *told* what to do, we feel empowered and respected. Choices give us a sense of autonomy and freedom. And when we experience power, respect, autonomy, and freedom, we tend to be more motivated and engaged.

Reflect on Choice in Your Own Writing

Let's be clear. There are times when we teachers aren't given much choice when it comes to the writing we do. Report card comments, class newsletters, and learning goals—these are just some of the writing experiences that are part of being a teacher.

Yet, even within these somewhat constrained writing tasks, there is still a bit of choice embedded. How will you word the comments you add on the report cards? In what format will you communicate to families? How will you structure and develop your personal learning goals?

In your life as a writer outside of school, choice abounds. That thank-you note you wrote to your neighbor? Chances are, you chose the paper and pen that you used. You also made choices about where you sat to write the thank-you note—on the couch, at the kitchen table, or at a desk. Choice permeates much of the writing we do as adults—choice of paper, choice of writing utensil, choice of topic, choice of audience. It's this choice that enlivens our work and gives us energy and enthusiasm.

Chances are, if someone told you, "Sit *here*. Use *this* paper. Write about *this* topic for *this* long using *this* writing utensil," I'm guessing your energy, engagement, and motivation would wither. And yet, sadly, this is exactly what many kids experience day in and day out in the writing classroom. We often ask students to engage in the complex (and sometimes difficult) task of writing without offering much choice at all. Meanwhile, we scratch our heads, wondering why some of our students appear to be so reluctant to write.

Don Graves put it this way: "Without realizing it, we wrest control away from the children and place roadblocks that thwart their intentions. Then we say, 'They don't want to write. What is a good way to motivate them?'" (quoted in Newkirk and Kittle 2013, 219).

What Does This Look Like in the Classroom?

When I arrive in Macie Harris' bright and cheerful kindergarten classroom, the kids are sitting in a semicircle on the floor. I've been invited in to teach them how to plan out their informational writing using sketches. After a brief lesson and a time to consider and talk about their own plans with a partner, I send the kids off to write. A flurry of activity ensues.

I watch as kids make their way to a corner of the room where different kinds of paper, clipboards, and every sort of writing utensil are stored. Some kids choose paper with a box at the top and lines below; some choose plain white paper; and some choose half-sheets of paper. Several kids reach for sharpened pencils from a bright container on the counter while others choose ballpoint pens or black fine-tip markers. A few kids grab small containers filled with sharp and brightly colored pencils.

I watch as several students pick up a clipboard and settle in on the floor around the classroom. A few kids make their way to tables that have been shortened so that the surface is the perfect height for a kindergartner to write on while kneeling. I notice that others have settled in to work at more traditional-looking tables scattered around the classroom.

Within moments, an engaged hum settles over the classroom. I marvel at how quickly the kids made these choices and settled into writing with enthusiasm and energy.

As I watch this all take place, it becomes clear to me that what I am witnessing is the result of good teaching and implicit trust in children. From day one, Macie has taught these five-year-olds about the choices they can make as writers. And she has trusted them to make these choices.

Later that evening, I send Macie an email, thanking her for opening up her classroom to me. I mention that, during my time in her classroom, I didn't see any student who was unmotivated to write. Every single one of her students dove into their writing with urgency, purpose, and even *joy*. "How did that happen?" I ask.

Macie responds: "I have quickly discovered that getting student buy-in is the whole essence of my teaching. Giving my students lots of choices and providing consistency in modeling, excitement, and encouragement about writing from the person they trust the most (me) has helped the kids develop confidence in themselves and a passion for writing."

As teachers, it's *our* job to create writing classrooms where students experience the autonomy, freedom, and engagement that comes with choice.

We have the choice to do this.

Kids don't.

Giving students choice doesn't mean that we surrender all control and embrace chaos and anarchy in our classrooms. However, it does mean that we honor children and trust them to make choices about their writing and themselves as writers.

Here are a few examples of the kinds of choices we can provide to help writers experience energy, engagement, and *joy*.

Kids Choose Their Own Topics

After reading and analyzing several published informational posters, students in Rylee Meier's fourth-grade classroom had the opportunity to create their own informational posters on a topic *of their choice*.

The energy in the classroom was palpable as students used what they had learned to write and design their own posters to display around the school. Knowing that they were doing real-world work that would be shared with a real audience definitely contributed to the students' motivation, but Rylee also noticed that students were engaged and energized because they were allowed to tap into their own interests and choose their own topics.

Rylee's students still learned how to do this particular kind of writing (informational posters); they weren't given a choice in that. However, simply providing a little bit of choice (of topic as well as page layout and design) was all it took to excite even the most apathetic writers in her classroom.

Students chose their own topics and created informational posters.

Kids Choose the Form the Writing Will Take

Students in Ariann Hess-Headlee's fifth-grade classroom work in partnerships throughout the year to create a monthly family newsletter about what they are learning in math, writing, literacy, science, and social studies.

Once students have learned how to write in other forms (interviews, book or product reviews, poetry, etc.), they can choose what kind of article they would like to contribute to the newsletter. Ariann has noticed that even her students who usually appear to be reluctant approach this writing experience with excitement!

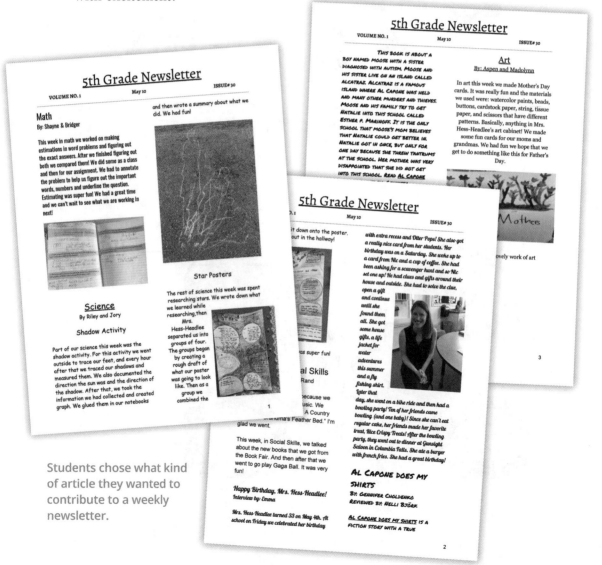

Students chose what kind of article they wanted to contribute to a weekly newsletter.

Kids Choose Who Will Read Their Writing

Kindergarten writers in Kristin Wild's classroom wrote reviews of the books they loved. When the reviews were finished, Kristen asked the students to think about where they might want to publish them.

Her students decided that the best place for their book reviews to be showcased was in the school library. Kristin took on the role of a copy editor and typed up the student reviews. These reviews, along with a photograph of each child holding their book, were displayed on the walls of the library so that students throughout the school could read the kindergarten book recommendations.

This experience was highly motivating because the students knew that their writing would be going public. And the students had a voice in the choice about who would be reading their writing. Bonus: Students throughout the school discovered some new books for their own reading!

Do you like sheep? Do you like rocket ships?

Then you should read this book called *Sheep Blast Off!*

It is where sheep get into a spaceship and blast off into space!

The teacher kept the student's language, but corrected spelling and added punctuation as needed to ensure that everyone could read the review.

Do you like sheep?
Do you like Rockit Ships?
Then you shood reed this
book calld Sheep Blast off
It is ware Sheep
get into a Spaseship
and Blast off into
spas!

Kids Choose Which Facts to Include in Their Writing

In Holly Hart's second-grade classroom, students learned how to write pieces meant to persuade a reader that their hometown was one of the best places to live. Together, students researched and gathered interesting facts that they could use to persuade the reader.

Some students, like Brady, chose to focus on the weather, safety, and favorite activities in their hometown. Other students chose to include facts and reasons that highlighted family-friendly activities, shopping, or schools in the area. Holly's students were all writing about the same topic, but they still had lots of choice in terms of what their finished product would look like and what facts they would include.

So, even though all of Holly's students were writing about the same topic, when it came time to write, students were able to make their own choices about which facts to include and how to organize those facts and infuse them into their pieces in a way that would engage the reader. Just that little bit of choice yielded a huge payoff for all of Holly's students—even those who sometimes appeared to be reluctant.

One more thing to note: Holly also allowed students to decide how long the piece of writing should be. Rather than saying something like, *You have to write at least two pages*, she let her student writers choose how long the piece would be.

Lifeless, contrived, and formulaic writing that is devoid of choice leads to lifeless, contrived, and formulaic writing pieces (and a slew of unmotivated writers). If students simply comply with an assignment in which the topic, form, and process have all been chosen for them, should we really be surprised when kids aren't super excited to write?

If, on the other hand, we give students choices—more voice, power, and ownership in their writing and in their writing process—motivation soars.

mountain bikes and/or road bikes.
There are also great camping sites.
Hyalite is close to Bozeman, and it's
by a river and a lake. Bozeman
really is the best place to
live

Kalispell   Bozeman

Bozeman is the Best Place to Live
Do you hate cloudy days? Do you think
they make you depressed? Well, if so, then you
might want to move to Bozeman, MT. Bozeman
averages 300 days of sun a year! Bozeman
is the best place to live. First of all, Bozeman
is the best place to live because it is a
friendly, safe, and clean community. People
will always say hi to you and do kind
things for you. Plus, Bozeman is a very
safe place. There are no gangs, not too
much crime, and certainly no gambling!
And there's no cigarettes (at most
places), and few casinos! Secondly, Bozeman

page ____1____

Ch. 5 p. 7

Students chose what facts to
infuse into their persuasive
writing.

is the best place to live because
there are many great restaurants.
First, there is Pizza Hut. Pizza
Hut has a great pizza bar and great
pizza! There is also Qdoba. Qdoba has
great tacos, lots of choices, and great
burrito bowls. Mackenzie River Pizza
has good salads, and it is known for
its superb pizza. Finally, Bozeman is the
best place to live because there
are lots of outdoor activities you
can do. There is hiking. You can hike up
the Drinking Horse or the "M" trails.
There are also lots of biking trails for

page ____2____

The standard doesn't say that students *must* include a precise number of reasons. In fact, it doesn't require that students follow a rigid guideline or formula at all. It simply asks that students support their view with reasons. How they do that can be left up to the writer.

CCSS.ELA-LITERACY.W.3.1
"Write opinion pieces on topics or texts, supporting a view with reasons."

The standard doesn't tell us *which* topic or text students should be writing about. I see room here for *students* to choose the topic or text about which to write an opinion piece.

CCSS.ELA-LITERACY.W.3.1.A
"Introduce the topic or text they are writing about, state an opinion, and create an organizational structure that lists reasons."

"Organizational structure" here does not automatically mean five-paragraph essay or "Use an Oreo cookie to structure the writing." In fact, as I read the standard, it seems to be inviting *students* to *create* their own organizational structure rather than follow a rigid, prescribed structure given to them by the teacher. By examining well-written opinion pieces (mentor texts), students can discover lots of different ways that writers create an organizational structure that lists reasons. Then students can *choose* their own structure!

This doesn't mean that students must use *certain* linking words and phrases or that *all* opinions must be connected with linking words and phrases. It means that linking words and phrases should be *one* method students use to establish an orderly flow of ideas. By examining quality opinion pieces (mentor texts), students can see all of the different words and phrases that writers use to connect opinions and then choose the ones that *they* feel would work best in their piece of writing.

CCSS.ELA-LITERACY.W.3.1.B
"Provide reasons that support the opinion."

CCSS.ELA-LITERACY.W.3.1.C
"Use linking words and phrases (e.g., *because, therefore, since, for example*) to connect opinions and reasons."

CCSS.ELA-LITERACY.W.3.1.D
"Provide a concluding statement or section."

Notice it does *not* say, "Provide a concluding statement that begins, 'In conclusion.'" A concluding statement might be a call to action for the reader. It might be a shocking fact or personal story. Embedded in this standard is choice: *Students* can decide if they'd like a statement or an entire section of writing to serve as the conclusion. And *they* can choose what that conclusion sounds like. Again, quality opinion pieces (mentor texts) can expose student writers to the myriad of ways that writers wrap up a piece of opinion writing.

Reality Check: *Standards and Rigor*

In my work with teachers across the country, I sometimes hear a narrative that goes like this: "Teaching and learning used to be so fun for teachers and kids. But now, everything is standards, standards, standards." It doesn't have to be that way.

When we look at state and national standards, we can easily see what skills we need to teach. However, the standards do not dictate *everything*. In fact, I would argue that most state and national standards have *choice* embedded in them; we, as teachers, get to *choose* how we teach the skills presented in the standards. We are given autonomy and ownership and power and choice when it comes to *how* we teach the standards.

When I look closely at state and national standards, not only do I discover that I have choice as a teacher in terms of how I teach, but I also see ample room for student choice!

Let's take a look at some Common Core State Standards for grade 3 (NGA Center for Best Practices and CCSSO 2010).

Nowhere in these standards does it tell us to give the students a topic about which to write. I don't find any standard that forces students to use a particular writing paper or utensil. There aren't firm parameters on how long a piece of writing should be. And, try as I may, I see *no* standard for any grade level that requires students to create a piece of writing that is structured into a traditional five-paragraph essay. Instead, the standards lay out skills that can be taught while still allowing for student choice and voice. I think choice is the key that unlocks students' motivation to engage in all of the complexities of skills that are represented in the standards.

How Can We Give Students Opportunities to Make Choices?

In my work with students I've found that even the smallest choice can have a big impact on the energy and excitement that students bring to writing. When teachers let kids take ownership of their writing and themselves as writers, kids have a much more positive attitude toward writing.

So, how can we give our students more voice and choice in the writing classroom? How can we use these powerful tools to motivate and engage the less-than-enthusiastic writers in our classroom?

In the following list, I've highlighted several simple ways to offer kids more choice in their writing experiences. As you read them, reflect on your own classroom and think about how you might use them, along with some ideas of your own.

- **Give kids choice of writing paper and writing utensils.** Many teachers find that it's helpful to allocate a shelf, counter, or table that can serve as a space to store all kinds of writing materials. Here, kids can find a variety of writing paper, styles, and sizes. This area also becomes a place to store all kinds of writing utensils: pens, pencils, colored pencils, and black fine-tip markers. These seemingly small choices can help students reinvest in their work with joy. If students have easy access to technology, you can also offer tablets, Chromebooks, or laptops to students during writing time.

- **Let students choose where to write.** Allowing students to find a space to write that works for them can also be helpful. Perhaps you have a comfy couch in your room where students might cozy up with a clipboard or other hard surface on which they can write. Some students might prefer to lie on their stomachs on the floor, while others might prefer to sit at a table in a more traditional posture. (See page 44 for more about flexible seating.)

  Giving kids just this little bit of choice—of power over their writing and themselves as writers—can have a huge payoff.

  Side Note: Some teachers worry that kids won't be able to be productive if teachers let them choose where to sit. If you notice that, for a few students, a certain seating arrangement isn't working for them, you can respectfully and discreetly address this in a one-on-one conversation. Simply help the child find a more productive place to write and then give the student another chance to make their own choice the next day.

● **Provide choice within parameters.** Recently, my husband and I were looking to replace the carpet in our bedroom. So on a snowy Saturday afternoon, we stopped by the carpet store to pick out the new carpet. When I entered the showroom and saw the vast amount of carpet samples, I froze. The overwhelming number of options caused me to immediately feel overwhelmed. Just moments earlier, on the way to the carpet store, my husband and I had chatted excitedly, thinking about what new carpet would do to our bedroom space. But the excitement quickly vanished once I encountered the seemingly endless options.

Sometimes too much choice can feel overwhelming. When this happens, we don't experience engagement and excitement. We often feel paralyzed.

Loren, the salesperson who was helping us, picked up on our unease. "Tell me a little bit about yourselves. Do you have kids? Pets?" he asked. We told him about our two rambunctious sons and our mini schnauzer. "It sounds like you are looking for a carpet that will last a long time and be durable while at the same time look nice," he said. "Am I right?"

We nodded.

"OK," he continued. "Let me take you over to this section of the showroom. Here you'll find the carpets that work well with kids and pets."

A noticeable change came over me. I felt calmer. A bit of that initial excitement came back as I perused the smaller section of carpet samples. I still had choices, but the choices had been narrowed a bit so that I didn't feel so overwhelmed.

Motivation, energy, empowerment, and engagement all hinge on choice. But choice can also be paralyzing.

So, in the writing classroom, offer choices within manageable parameters. For example, in kindergarten and first grade, start out by giving students two or three choices of paper. Over the course of the school year, you can add more options. For upper grades, consider narrowing the choices of writing form. Students can start out with two choices: create a PowerPoint presentation or a brochure. Over time, as kids become more confident in their ability as writers, you can give them more choices.

● **When possible, let kids choose topics that interest them.** I'm not suggesting that you *never* give students a topic about which to write. But I have found that, when possible, it is empowering for students to choose topics that are of interest to *them*. When I work with student (and adult) writers, I often ask them to place one hand on their head and the other hand on their heart. *Write about what you* know *about and* care *about. When you write about what you know about and care about, you'll have a lot to say.* It's true. We tend to write more and write better when we are writing on a topic about which we are passionate.

There are times when you might choose to narrow topics so that students are writing in a particular genre or form. But within that narrow focus, you can still give students some choice. For example, if you're learning about the seven continents as part of your content study in social studies—learning about the climates, economy, and people groups of each continent—you can teach students how to write informational pieces related to what they are learning in social studies. However, you can still provide choices within that topic: Perhaps students can choose to write about the continent that would be most interesting to them. Or students can choose to focus in on a particular subtopic, such as the people groups in that continent.

If you're learning about weather in science and students are focusing on opinion or persuasive writing, students could create persuasive posters about how to stay safe during a particular type of extreme weather. You've chosen the topic (weather) and the writing genre (persuasive), but students are choosing what kind of extreme weather they will write about (blizzards, hurricanes, thunderstorms, etc.).

- **Allow flexibility when it comes to process**. We don't want to crush the energy and interest of writers by asking them to follow a rigid series of steps as they write. In earlier grades, being rigid about process might look like insisting that kids draw before they write or write before they draw. In upper-elementary classrooms, this may look like following a strict interpretation of "*the* Writing Process" or insisting on a specific and prescribed method of prewriting, such as using a graphic organizer. No matter what grade you're teaching, the solution is the same: let them choose. If a student gets stuck or needs support, confer with them and help them move forward.

  Following rigid steps doesn't make you a stronger writer; it makes you good at following rigid steps. So don't be a stickler when it comes to your own writing process or how you think the process should go. Put the kids in the driver's seat and let them find a process that works for them. For some kids, sketching first and then writing might prove to be helpful. For other kids, writing long and fast might help them get their ideas down. Some kids find that talking before they write helps. For others, a simple planning technique, like storyboarding, might be helpful.

  Showcase lots of different ways to go about writing and then let kids try them out and decide what is most helpful to them.

Recently, a teacher told me that she was changing the way she was teaching writing. Before, she had required all her students to write about the same topic in the very same way. Not surprisingly, her students were less than enthused. She knew something needed to change.

She started by releasing some control and letting her students make choices about paper, utensils, topic, and process. She began to see a huge difference in her students. Instead of groaning when it was time for writing, her students begged to write each day. The quality of the students' writing improved, too. She started to see each child's personality bloom on the page.

"I realized that I could have continued making all of my students do cookie-cutter kinds of writing, where each piece pretty much looked the same because I was controlling everything," she said. "But that's not where the magic happens. The magic happens when I trust kids and let go of some control."

Now it's your turn! What are some other ways you could give kids more choice in the writing experiences in your classroom?

Just to get the ball rolling, here are some questions I consider to ensure that writing experiences include student choice.

- **What am I trying to teach?** Am I teaching a particular craft move? A particular form of writing? If I'm teaching a specific craft move like how to write a powerful introduction to an opinion piece, it doesn't mean that students all need to write about the same topic. I can teach them how to craft a powerful introduction using whatever topic is a passion for them; a powerful introduction is a powerful introduction. If I'm focusing my teaching on a particular writing form like a procedural text, we don't all need to write about the same topic (how to tie a shoe or how to make a PB and J). My students can still learn about the structure and features of a procedural text while writing on a topic about which they are an expert.

- **If the topic needs to be narrowed, how can I still provide choice within that narrowed topic?** For example, if I'm integrating our science content into writing and we're all going to be writing about landforms, I can still provide some choice within that topic. Perhaps students can decide what form their writing might take: an informational poster, a brochure, or an electronic slideshow. Or students could focus their writing on a particular landform of their choosing.

How Can We Leverage the Power of Choice?

Are you starting to think about how choice might unlock the engagement and excitement about writing in your classroom?

Once you've made some room for student choice and voice, you are ready to consider one more question: How can you maximize the immense power that choice can have on all kids in your classroom? Let's look at some suggestions.

1. **Start with real-world models.**

There is real power in using mentor texts in the classroom. When I show my students what *real, published* writers do in their work, it helps them see what's possible in their own writing. It gives them options to choose from, but it also helps them to see that there is a wide range of options beyond what I'm showing them.

To help students get to know these varied texts, we read *through the eyes of a writer.* For instance, if I'm teaching kids to include diagrams in their informational writing, I can show them the different kinds of diagrams that published writers include in their books. If I'm teaching students how to write a review of a favorite product, I will show them real-world examples of product reviews online. Or if students are creating a blog or a vlog, I can show them the finished products that other writers have produced. When students see what it could look like (or sound like) when it's finished, it helps them cast a vision for what's possible in their writing and helps them know what they are aiming for in terms of a finished product. With this in mind, they can make purposeful and intentional choices.

So, how can we use real-world models to teach students about choice and voice in their own writing?

Let's start with something simple like page layout. Writers make a lot of choices when it comes to how each of their pages is designed. You can show students this by gathering a few published books from the school library or your classroom library. You don't need to spend too much time combing through the books word by word—just make sure that the texts you choose showcase a variety of page layouts.

Invite students to join you in closely examining the layout of a few pages from each book. You and your students may notice that, on one page, the writer has chosen to put text on the right side of the page with a photograph on the left. On the next page you might notice that the same author created a two-page spread with a large diagram spanning the pages and only short bits of text on the bottom. As you and your students flip to yet another page, you might see a heading, a large section of text with multiple paragraphs, and a visual such as a map on the right-hand side of the page.

Ask students to consider *why* the author used a variety of page layouts throughout the book. Together, you and your students might notice that the writer, along with the publishing team, made a plethora of choices about how the pages would look. These choices were all made with the *reader* in mind. Making each page visually pleasing helps keep a reader's interest.

Page layout is just one example of the kinds of choices real writers make. Consider revisiting the same few texts, but this time pay close attention to the myriad of other choices this writer made before, during, and after writing the text.

These choices likely included

- the topic
- which facts to include
- the format
- which visuals to add to support the text
- the length of text, the structure of text, and the type of words included in the text.

2. **Think aloud as you make choices before you write.**

While it can be helpful for students to see how published writers make choices and how those choices impact the finished products, there's an even greater impact when students watch a mentor writer (that's you) make choices before, during, and after writing. It's one thing to *tell* our students about the choices a published author has made. It's another thing to *show* our students what this looks like in real time. I've found that when students first observe *me* making choices about *my* writing, confidence, engagement, and enjoyment all improve. It's fascinating (and extremely helpful) to see and hear how another writer gets an idea from his or her head onto the page.

Let's take the choice of topic, for example. Thinking aloud as you model and make choices about topic might sound something like this: *Over the past few days we've learned a lot about informational writing. Now, it's time for us to write! Watch me as I start my own piece. Watch as I think about topics that are important to me. And*

*then watch as I choose a topic about which I can write. Let's see . . .
what am I an expert on? Well, I know a lot about adopting a dog.
Our family adopted a dog from the shelter 3 years ago. I could write
a piece about rescue dogs and how to adopt them and bring them
into your family. Or maybe I could write about cooking. I do a lot of
cooking, so I guess I'm becoming an expert on that. Or, I love to go
to the public library and choose a new book to read. Maybe I could
write a piece to teach others how to choose a book. I think I'll write
a piece all about rescue dogs—how to adopt them and bring them
into your family.*

If I struggle a little bit in choosing a topic, that's even better!
Making choices as a writer isn't always easy. When I make this
invisible process (and struggle) visible to students (especially to
writers who might appear to be reluctant), they begin to understand
that no one has some sort of magical pixie dust of inspiration
descend on them. Writers simply struggle through and make lots and
lots of choices.

3. Show students how you make choices as you write.

Rest assured that it's not necessary for you to write your entire piece
in front of students. However, most teachers find it helpful to write at
least a small portion of the piece in front of the kids each day. That
way, you can think aloud daily and let your students see that, as you
write, you're constantly making choices. For example:

- *How shall I begin?*
- *How do I want to design this page of text?*
- *What word do I want to use here?*
- *Should I simply write facts about this topic?
  Or should I add something that will connect
  with the reader on an emotional level?*
- *What kind of visual do I want to add here?*
- *What have I learned from other authors that I
  can add to my piece?*

Let your students see (and hear) you work through questions like these and make choices. In doing so, you are showing students how you make choices and take ownership of your writing.

4. **Coach individual writers**.

Choice is a powerful component when we coach writers one-on-one as well. The simple act of coming alongside a student communicates that you value and appreciate them as an individual. The fact that you're taking time out of the instructional day to work one-on-one with students shows students that individuals matter to you.

Here are tips to help you coach writers as you work with them:

• **See the child as a unique individual.** When you embrace handing over choices to the students in your classroom, what you're

really saying is that you understand that students are unique, complex individuals. That's why coaching and conferring with individual writers is so powerful. If you have twenty-five students in your classroom, this means you have twenty-five different writers with varying degrees of skills, confidence levels, and misconceptions and beliefs about writing and themselves as writers. As I confer with individual kids about the choices they are making, I learn things not just about the *writer* but about the *child*. What interests them? What history and stories are they bringing to their writing work? When I know the children well, I can be much more effective in motivating them.

• **Be prepared to support students who can't decide.** Some kids—especially kids who might not be accustomed to making choices and thinking about options for their own writing—might have trouble making choices or even generating some options. When I'm working with a student who is experiencing this, I typically try the following:

1. **Think alongside them.** I sit next to the student, close my eyes, and think with them. I often say something like, *I'll think alongside you for a minute or two. Sometimes, when another writer thinks with you, it can be helpful.*

2. **Provide some alone think-time.** If, after a minute or two, the student is still struggling, I offer them some time to think on their own. I say, *I'm going to go work with other writers for a couple of minutes. I'll check back with you after you've had some quiet time to think.*

3. **Invite them to join me on a gallery walk.** If, after a few minutes of thinking, the student is still struggling, I invite them to walk around the room with me. Together, we peek over the shoulders of other students to see what they've done. Sometimes, I approach a table of writers and say, *Pardon the interruption, writers. We are doing a gallery walk to see what topics others are writing about [or how other writers began their narratives, or whatever is tripping up the student who is struggling]. Can you tell us what you're doing?*

4. **Provide a bit more alone think-time.** If the child is *still* struggling to come up with something, I give the child another minute or two to think quietly on their own while I continue to confer with other students.

   If, after offering think-time and time to learn from other writers in the classroom, the student is still stuck, I might go ahead and make the choice for the student and ask them to get started. I recommend doing this only when the child is becoming distressed about not being able to make a choice. In my twenty-six years of working with students, I've had to do this only twice.

- **Ask questions.** When I approach a writer and his piece of writing with curiosity and wonder, I'm communicating an important message: *I see what you've done on the page. But I'm much more interested in the thinking that's behind the words on the page.* Here are a few questions to get the conversation going:

  - *Tell me how you came up with this topic.*
  - *Wow! I can tell you know a lot about this topic.*
  - *How did you become such an expert on this topic?*
  - *Tell me about the choice to place your text here and the visual support over here. What were you thinking?*

  These simple questions pack a powerful punch. You're reinforcing the belief that writers make choices and that you're curious about the choices that this particular writer made. When you show genuine interest, you're saying, "You're interesting to me. I'm interested not just in what you are writing but also in *you* as a writer and the thinking that goes into your writing."

- **Call the student a writer.** Simply say, *You're the writer,* or *This is* your *writing.* Sometimes I find that students are a bit taken aback by this idea of choice, especially if they haven't had very many experiences with being allowed to choose their own topic or have ownership in their writing. Sometimes students have endured a steady diet of writing assignments in which they were told what to write about, what formula or structure to use, and how long it needed to be. They simply aren't accustomed to making choices. So use this one-on-one conversation to reiterate the choices that students have. For example, you might nudge a student to try something or give them an idea to consider including in their writing. However, when you do this, be quick to follow it up with something like, *That's just an idea. You* are *the writer. This is* your *piece of writing. You* get the final say. I use these phrases a lot as I'm conferring. This is intentional. I want to convey the message that, while we all may be doing the same kind of writing work, *that child* is the writer. *They* have control and ownership over the words on the page.

Closing Thoughts

Ours is a culture that values choice.

This is true when we order coffee.

This should be true in our writing classrooms.

When we give our students some choice about what to write and how to write it, the message we are sending is clear: *I trust you. I respect you. I value what you bring to this work. Your perspective matters. Your voice matters. You matter.*

If we want writers to move from reluctant to recharged, we need to create classroom environments and writing experiences that give students choice. Choice helps students to feel empowered and respected. And when students feel empowered and respected, they tend to be more motivated and engaged in the work.

I've listed some questions to consider as you take a reflective and honest look at your current practices in the hope of engaging all of your students.

If you're reading this book with a group of colleagues, use these questions to guide your shared conversation and learning.

Questions for Reflection

1. Am I allowing my students to make choices when they engage in writing? Or am I making most of the decisions in terms of writing topics, assignments, and form?

2. What might I lose if I let go of some of the control in terms of writing? What might I gain?

3. How can I provide my students some choice with structure?

4. What choices might be highly motivating to my less-than-enthusiastic writers?

Chapter Six

Maintain a Healthy Perspective on Conventions

*Students won't pay attention to conventions
if they don't care about the writing. When they write with a
valued reader in mind, they take conventions seriously, even in
a first draft. They come to understand that conventions are a
necessity that make the text readable.*

—Regie Routman

Have you ever wondered if you struggle with control? Here's a simple and foolproof way to find out: Bake with young children.

Since my kids were small, I have invited them into the kitchen, provided a stool (so they could reach the countertop), and attempted to bake. I did this for lots of reasons: I wanted my boys to be comfortable in the kitchen—to see it not as an off-limits, Mom-only part of the house, but a gathering place where memories (and maybe some almost edible cookies) could be made. I also wanted to bake with my kids because there's something special about the shared experience of taking a slew of raw ingredients and turning them into something new and different.

But I have to admit I am a bit of a control freak.

So inviting small beings into my fairly organized and relatively clean kitchen proved to be a bit of a challenge. OK—a massive challenge.

I found myself tensing up when watching my sons crack eggs or measure (not so precisely) that cup of flour. As an adult who has been baking for a good number of years, I've grown to be fairly precise in my measuring and recipe following. Baking with my kids required me to relax a bit on the "rules of baking" so that we could enjoy the *process*. I came to realize that it wasn't as important that they followed the recipe *exactly* or that they measured *correctly*. Give or take a little bit would be OK, as long as they would discover a love of baking or spending time in the kitchen creating something to be shared with others.

Don't get me wrong. There were a few basic and nonnegotiable principles that I knew I needed to teach them: Don't eat raw eggs. Wash your hands before you begin. You can't substitute salt for sugar. There are standard units of measurement that we use when we bake. It's imperative that you add a half *teaspoon* of salt rather than a half *cup* of salt.

But if I wanted to help my boys grow into men who would know their way around a kitchen (and how to make a decent batch of chocolate chip cookies), I needed to hold these two goals in tension: teach them the basic rules of baking *and* help them enjoy the process of baking. If I focused too heavily on the rules and on baking *correctly*, my kids might learn how to bake, but it's unlikely that they would enjoy it and choose to continue baking.

I wonder if learning to write is a little bit like learning to bake? I think we could all agree that our goal for the kids in our classroom is that they grow and evolve into joyfully literate adults who use writing to impact and influence the world around them. However, if we develop and foster an unhealthy perspective on conventions—if we take on the role of perfectionistic rule followers who demand that everything our students write be *correct*—we might unknowingly quench the spark of engagement and joy.

Don Graves, the father of most of what we know about effective and powerful writing instruction, put it this way:

Most teaching of writing is pointed toward the eradication of error, the mastery of minute, meaningless components that make little sense to the child. Small wonder. Most language arts texts, workbooks, computer software, and reams of behavioral objectives are directed toward the "easy" control of components that will show more specific growth. Although some growth may be evident on components, rarely does it result in the child's use of writing as a tool for learning and enjoyment. Make no mistake, component skills are important; if children do not learn to spell or use a pencil to get words on paper, they won't use writing for learning any more than the other children drilled on component skills. The writing-process approach simply stresses meaning first, and then skills in the context of meaning. (1985)

In Graves' words we see that the same beautiful tension that I experienced in baking holds true in writing as well. We want kids to develop the skills they'll need to write well but not at the expense of making meaning and definitely not at the expense of engagement and enjoyment of the *process*.

Conventions matter. They do. Conventions exist out of respect for the reader. If writing has strong, sound conventions, the reader can focus on the content in the piece. When a piece of writing is riddled with errors in conventions, the reader becomes distracted from the *meaning* of the piece.

Correct use of conventions is important to a piece of writing, but conventions aren't *everything*. In addition to strong conventions, a strong piece of writing is clear and organized. It sounds fluent, rather than choppy or forced, when read aloud. The words are precise, rich, and powerful, creating a picture in the reader's mind. And strong writing has voice. It connects with a reader on an emotional level. It surprises, emotes, or makes someone laugh. When you read a strong piece of writing, the writer's personality comes through on the page. Yes, conventions are important, but they aren't the *only* component that's needed to create quality writing.

Our challenge as teachers of writing is to strike a healthy balance between teaching conventions and *overemphasizing* them and thus quenching the enjoyment of writing.

Note: Throughout this chapter, I use the term *conventions*. Let's make sure that we are all thinking about the same thing when I use that term. Conventions, in the way that I am using the term in this chapter, are anything that a professional proofreader would attend to: punctuation, capitalization, spelling, and grammar.

Reflect on Your Own Life as a Writer

Cast your mind back to the types of writing you have done in the last few days. I'm not talking about the writing you've done in your classroom with your kids, but writing you've done as a regular person and literate adult.

I'll go first.

I wrote a thank-you email to my son's fourth-grade teacher to thank her for a smooth start to the school year. I wrote loads and loads and loads of emails. I sent a few dozen texts. And I compiled a massive to-do list to help me remember everything that I needed to get done this week.

OK. It's your turn. What types of writing have you done this week? Is your list similar to mine?

Now I'm wondering: Were your conventions correct in each and every type of writing you composed?

As I think back to the writing that I did this week, the answer would be it depends. When I wrote that email to a principal at a school I'm currently supporting, I slowed down as I typed and carefully considered my spelling, grammar, and punctuation. Once I wrote the email, I reread it to make sure I hadn't made any gross errors in conventions. But that to-do list? Well, that's another story. As long as I could read it, I wasn't too concerned if it was correct or not. I'm guessing that if every piece of writing I did this week were going to be evaluated, scrutinized, and corrected by someone to make sure it was all conventionally precise, I probably wouldn't have wanted to write at all.

Conventions count—just not all the time. As regular people outside of school, we understand that the main purpose of writing is to communicate, to help us remember, to inform, to give instructions, and to share our opinions. As adults, we understand that conventions support the content. If the conventions are too far off the mark, the reader won't understand our message. But not every piece of writing we do needs to go through the sieve of correctness when it comes to conventions. And I'm guessing that if someone were looking over our shoulder each time we wrote to make sure that everything was correct, we probably would find something else—anything else—to do *except* write.

Picture what would happen if my husband looked at my scribbled grocery list sitting on the kitchen counter and announced, "That's not how you spell *asparagus*. You'll need to fix that." First of all, those words would probably start a fight. Well, not a fight. In our house we call it "intense fellowship." Also, I can assure you that I would be more hesitant and reluctant to write in the future. To be honest, I would think, "Never mind. I'll just see if I can remember my list of groceries in my head. I'm not going through *that* again."

Don Graves put it this way: "When a child writes, 'My sister was hit by a terck yesterday.' and the teacher's response is a red-circled 'terck' with no further comment, educational standards may have been upheld but the child will think twice before entering the writing process again. Inane and apathetic writing is often the writer's only means of self-protection" (quoted in Newkirk and Kittle 2013, 22).

My point here is that, sometimes we, as well-meaning teachers, *overemphasize* conventions when our students write. Our heart is in the right place. We simply want our students to become proficient writers. We require (or even *demand*) that everything our students write be correct, which is interesting because we don't hold ourselves to this same standard. Our grocery list doesn't have to be spelled perfectly, but the email to our insurance agent does.

What Does This Look Like in the Classroom?

I'm not suggesting that we take all of the conventions of language and throw them in the trash. I'm not suggesting we stand on our desk and announce in a loud voice, *Conventions don't matter, kids! Simply write from your heart!*

What I am suggesting is that we put conventions in their proper place and make sure that being correct isn't the only goal our students have as writers.

In the following sections, I've listed a few examples of what maintaining a healthy perspective on conventions might look like in the classroom.

Kids and Teachers Engage in Conversations About the Qualities of Good Writing

In some classrooms, teachers have a conversation with their students about the characteristics of quality writing. To get the conversation going, the teacher asks, *What makes good writing?* Kids often respond to this question by saying the following:

- *It's long.*

- *It has neat handwriting.*

- *Everything is spelled correctly.*

Responses like this show that, somewhere along the way, kids learned to equate good writing with factors that have nothing to do with the quality of the writing. These kinds of responses give us an opening into a conversation about what really matters in writing.

Once kids have had a chance to share their thinking, the teacher shares a few short but strong pieces of writing. The pieces are funny, poignant, moving, or thought-provoking. After the teacher shares the pieces, she asks her students, *What did you like about these pieces? What did you notice?* Students share their thinking with a partner while she listens in, and then she records their observations.

The kids say things like:

- *It's funny!*

- *The words are interesting.*

- *You can picture the whole thing in your head while you read it.*

- *It makes you* feel *something.*

At the end of this experience, the teacher asks students to look carefully at the list of the characteristics they've created. She explains that strong writing is made up of a variety of features. It's not *just* the conventions that matter; it's the *content*! This helps kids who see themselves as lacking in one dimension of writing (like spelling or grammar) realize that writing has more than one dimension.

Kids Have Freedom with Paper and Format

Lisa Miller, a first-grade teacher at Lincoln Elementary, told me about Jesamie, a student who typically produced little writing. Lisa noticed that, when she was asked to write, Jesamie would become hesitant to put her words down on paper. After learning more about a balanced approach to conventions, Lisa had a hunch about what was holding Jesamie back. "This sweet writer was being held back by my focus on conventions and wanting her paper to be perfect or to fit the template of the writing paper I had given her! If the writing paper had two lines, she would fill them with two perfect sentences and then announce that she was done. I decided to try giving her blank paper instead. It was just what this writer needed: 'permission' from me to not focus so much on the perfect sentence (or two), but to put down her thoughts in any format she wanted to. Now, Jesamie is a student who truly *loves* to write. This small change was a *game changer* for her."

Kids Learn Conventions in Context

If you've taught for any length of time, you've probably learned what *doesn't* work when it comes to teaching things like grammar, punctuation, spelling, and capitalization: teaching conventions in isolation by using either worksheets or workbooks. The problem with teaching conventions this way is that the conventions are decontextualized. The skill is pulled out of real reading and writing and placed on a worksheet or workbook page; it's not connected to actual reading or writing. Kids might be able to complete the worksheet or workbook page and get

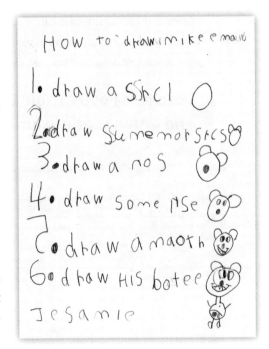

What struck me first about Jesamie's writing is the sheer volume of it! This is a writer who, before Lisa gave her a blank piece of paper, was doing the bare minimum of writing required. I also noticed that Jesamie has not focused so much on getting the perfect sentence down. Instead, she has focused on making sure her directions were clear to the reader. She's added numbered steps and a picture to go along with each step. She's also used brave spelling to get down the sounds she heard in the words she was writing.

most of the answers correct, but the skill on that worksheet simply doesn't transfer into the students' writing. Students can "master" that skill out of context, but if you ask them to infuse this skill into their writing, it falls apart.

So, when I'm invited in to help kids learn a particular convention, like punctuation, I teach it as part of an explicit minilesson. Then, as students go off to write, I can encourage the kids to practice that skill in whatever they are working on in writing that day. This helps reengage writers because—let's face it—very few of us enjoy filling out a workbook page. We're much more motivated to engage in meaningful writing and then learn how a skill (like punctuation) can make our writing stronger. And less-than-enthusiastic writers start to grasp that conventions exist out of respect for the reader, not just to get a sticker, smiley face, or percentage grade on the worksheet.

Teachers Focus Their Observations and Conversations on *One* Convention at a Time

Student	I Can Use Punctuation	I Can Use Capital Letters
Jacob	• keep going	
Mason	help x2	teach beg.
William	| . .?	name✓ teach I
Sophia	· · ·! 'keep going	teach title, I
Isabella	• encourage!	beg, names, I
Emma	!!! try others	I , teach name
Jayden	✓!	✓ beg ✓
Noah	• change!	beg ✓
Michael	• encourage to try others	I, beg ✓
Ava	! • help	I ✓
Emily	!···| encourage	no pnc - encourage to try
Ethan	— !	— beg ✓ I ✓
Liam	• encourage to try another	beg of sentence name of City
Abby	— encourage to use	— —
Andrew	. !	encourage I ✓ beg of sentence
Grace	•! keep going	I
Samantha	! • keep going	title / beg of sent names
James	!? • keep going	
Lillian	•? keep going	• bulleted list

As the teacher checked in with each student, she saw who was applying the new learning and who might have needed more support.

In Karen Arnold's second-grade classroom, she identifies one type of convention on which she wants her students to focus, like capitalizing the beginning of a sentence. After she teaches a specific lesson on this skill, she tells her kids that she'll be coming around to admire them as they write and focus on this one thing.

As she circulates from kid to kid, she carries a clipboard with a class list on the left and the specific convention written at the top. Karen chats with each child briefly, checking in to see how kids are doing with capitalizing. Once she's checked in with each student, she can see who is applying this new learning and who might need more support. Even writers who appear very reluctant can feel empowered and energized because, as they write, they are focusing on just *one* convention, not the world of writing conventions.

Reality Check: *Standards and Rigor*

Let's face it. The majority of us are working under Common Core or other state standards when it comes to writing. Rather than viewing these standards as a major killjoy to teaching and learning, I find it helpful to use the standards to help me balance my instruction.

For instance, when I look at the Common Core writing standards (and most state standards), I notice that they are organized in a way that helps us maintain a healthy perspective on conventions. Let me show you what I mean. Here is a list of writing standards for grade 2, as found in the CCSS (NGA Center for Best Practices and CCSSO 2010).

CCSS.ELA-LITERACY.W.2.1
"Write opinion pieces in which they introduce the topic or book they are writing about, state an opinion, supply reasons that support the opinion, use linking words (e.g., *because, and, also*) to connect opinion and reasons, and provide a concluding statement or section."

CCSS.ELA-LITERACY.W.2.2
"Write informative/explanatory texts in which they introduce a topic, use facts and definitions to develop points, and provide a concluding statement or section."

CCSS.ELA-LITERACY.W.2.3
"Write narratives in which they recount a well-elaborated event or short sequence of events, include details to describe actions, thoughts, and feelings, use temporal words to signal event order, and provide a sense of closure."

CCSS.ELA-LITERACY.W.2.5
"With guidance and support from adults and peers, focus on a topic and strengthen writing as needed by revising and editing."

CCSS.ELA-LITERACY.W.2.6
"With guidance and support from adults, use a variety of digital tools to produce and publish writing, including in collaboration with peers."

CCSS.ELA-LITERACY.W.2.7
"Participate in shared research and writing projects (e.g., read a number of books on a single topic to produce a report; record science observations)."

CCSS.ELA-LITERACY.W.2.8
"Recall information from experiences or gather information from provided sources to answer a question."

I see standards that are focused on *text types* and *purposes*. I see standards that are focused on the *process* of writing and *distribution of writing*. And I see standards that focus on *researching* when writing.

Whoa. Wait a minute. Where are the conventions? It's interesting to note that in the CCSS (and most state standards), conventions aren't listed as part of the writing standards, but rather as *language* standards. As I examine the conventions of language that are spelled out in that section of the standards, I notice that teachers are prompted to think of these conventions in terms of *writing*, *speaking*, *reading*, or *listening*. In other words, many of the conventions of language (especially the ones that speak to grammar) are necessary when reading, listening, and speaking—not just when writing.

It's clear to me that the CCSS (and most state standards) assert that it's important for students to understand and master conventions but that we should keep these conventions in balance with other components of writing.

Let's take a look at the piece of writing shown in Figure 6.1, which was crafted by a second-grade student, and see how conventions are balanced with other characteristics of strong writing.

Figure 6.1

My Hero!(Cody)

It was a regular old recess. Or so I thought! The bell rang to 10:30 and I flew out the door, with Cody right behind me. Me and Cody made a beeline for the climbing tower. Little did I know that Cody was going to make a life-changing impact in my life. We were running to the climbing tower when suddenly.......

"WHAM!" I had slipped on the ice, going at least 10 mph! Luckilly, Cody was right behind me. He was brave enough to get a teacher right away. He took me in to the office. Cody was really optimistic! He told me if If I just got help quickly, I'd be fine! It turns out I had a broken wrist, but it was great that I got help quickly, or It could have been worse. That is why cody is my hero!!

CCSS.ELA-LITERACY.W.2.3
"Write narratives in which they recount a well-elaborated event or short sequence of events, include details to describe actions, thoughts, and feelings, use temporal words to signal event order, and provide a sense of closure."

Brady has recounted a "well-elaborated event" of the day he slipped on the ice and broke his wrist. He has also recalled information from this experience.

CCSS.ELA-LITERACY.L.2.1.D
"Form and use the past tense of frequently occurring irregular verbs (e.g., *sat, hid, told*)."

Brady has formed and used the past tense of the irregular verb *fly*.

CCSS.ELA-LITERACY.W.2.3

Brady has used some "temporal words" like *suddenly* and phrases like *the bell rang to 10:30* to signal event order.

CCSS.ELA-LITERACY.W.2.3

Brady has included details to describe the actions that took place during this fateful recess.

CCSS.ELA-LITERACY.L.2.2
"Demonstrate command of the conventions of standard English capitalization, punctuation, and spelling when writing."

In this piece, Brady's conventions are, for the most part, sound, which is appropriate for him as a second grader.

CCSS.ELA-LITERACY.W.2.3

He has provided a "sense of closure" for his reader.

How Can We Maintain a Healthy Perspective on Conventions?

So, how can we teach conventions well while at the same time keep them in a healthy balance with other, equally important goals for the writers in our class? How can we help students see that punctuation, spelling, capitalization, and grammar are their *allies*, not their *enemies*? How can we emphasize conventions without *overemphasizing* them?

Here are a few simple ways to approach all of these questions.

- **When it comes to punctuation, start them young!** I'm speaking here to primary teachers—those angels who teach kindergarten or first grade. My friends, you have been given a magical window of time in which kids are actually excited to learn a new kind of convention.

  My oldest son is in middle school. I have to confess that *not once* has my child skipped home from school excited to tell me that he learned how to use a semicolon. However, if you teach a kindergartner how to use an ellipsis (the three dots [. . .] that tell the reader that something is coming), they will announce their discovery to the *world*—their bus driver, their neighbors and their siblings. They will call aunts and uncles far and wide to share this new discovery.

  Capitalize on this beautiful window of joy and discovery! Show students *all kinds* of punctuation and then watch (and maybe even join in with) the excitement that ensues.

  Please don't misunderstand me here. You're not *expecting* that kindergartners and first graders use all forms of punctuation correctly. But go ahead and teach them anyway! If we start to introduce different kinds of punctuation early, perhaps students won't learn to *fear* them (and avoid writing) later on. Maybe they'll begin to make friends with punctuation, which might help them make friends with other kinds of conventions. Who knows? They just might fall in love with writing.

- **Celebrate discovery.** Sometimes, when you teach a student a new kind of convention, you might notice that the student *overuses* the convention at first. Anyone who teaches kindergarten or first grade has probably seen this: You show students how writers use periods in their writing. Then you write a bit of your piece in front of your students, thinking aloud about where you are placing a period and why. As you send the kids off to write and walk around to admire their work, you notice something: more than a few kids are placing a. period. after. every. word.

Have you seen this? Instead of going straight into the role of corrector-in-chief, take a deep breath and relax. Try saying something like this: *I see you've discovered periods. You're using them a lot in your writing!*

Most writing teachers agree that students tend to overuse a convention at first before they start to use it appropriately. Just as we celebrate and encourage a child who is learning to walk, through each faltering and teetering step, we want to celebrate a kid's first attempt at using more sophisticated conventions of language.

- **Engage in conversations about publishing levels.** In our everyday lives as adults who write, we create pieces of writing for a variety of readers and purposes. Not everything we write is polished and perfect when it comes to conventions. (If *everything* we wrote had to be that way, we would probably avoid writing altogether.)

  Bring in some writing from your own life and show kids how there are different expectations for different kinds of writing. That grocery list you scribbled on a sticky note doesn't need to be correct. It just needs to be readable. The note you left for your son to remind him to walk the dog doesn't have to be perfect, but your son needs to be able to read it. But that thank-you note you wrote to a veteran—*that* needs to be as close to perfect as you can get.

  Some teachers find that numbers help kids understand that the focus on conventions changes based on the reader. Consider posting these publishing levels on the wall of your classroom:

  Publishing Level 1: You and only you need to be able to read your writing.

  Publishing Level 2: Someone else needs to be able to read your writing.

  Publishing Level 3: Perfect, polished, and published work.

Once kids understand the different levels, you can simply tell kids what level you are expecting for different pieces of writing. For example, if you're starting a unit in math on fractions, you can ask kids to use their math learning log (a simple composition notebook) to write down what they already know about fractions. Then, you can simply say, "Publishing Level 2." When kids are crafting a poem to be showcased during the school's open house night, you can remind them that this should be Publishing Level 3 writing.

This kind of explanation helps all writers, but especially writers who may have fallen out of love with writing because of past instruction that focused too heavily on conventions or that required that *everything* students wrote be perfect.

- **Give students *time* before asking them to edit.** Can you relate to this scenario? You write a parent newsletter. Before you send it out, you proofread it a few times to make sure there are no glaring mistakes in punctuation, spelling, capitalization, and grammar. Once you're sure that it's ready to go, you send it out into the world. A few days later, you reread the newsletter and are mortified to see the mistakes that you missed! How did that happen? Didn't you proofread it a few times?

When the brain is too close to composing the text, it has a hard time seeing the mistakes. When we reread a piece *right after* we write it, it can look so perfect to us! The brain needs a little bit of distance and time from the piece before it can look at it with the eyes of an editor. Personally, I've found that, if I take a forty-eight- to seventy-two-hour break between when I write something and the time that I proofread it, it's easier to find the mistakes.

Writers who might appear to be reluctant, in particular, appreciate this brain break from their writing. Once they've had some time and distance from a piece, they are better equipped to make sure it's polished and ready for the world. When it's polished and ready for the world, the writer receives encouragement and maybe even *praise*. This leads to a more positive feeling about writing and a willingness to keep writing!

- **Publish wisely.** Throughout the year, there will be times when you'll want to share your students' writing with the world. For some writers who are hesitant, knowing that their work will be published and celebrated keeps them focused and engaged in the hard work of drafting, revising, and editing. So publish early and publish often!

  When your students are ready to publish level 3 writing pieces, they'll want to take some extra time to make sure their conventions are as sound as possible. Here are a couple of ways you can ensure that your students' writing is ready for an outside audience:

  - **Take on the role of a copy editor.** If your students have crafted *short* pieces of writing (like book reviews to be displayed in your town's public library), show them how to edit for a few conventions that you've explicitly taught. After students have done what they can in terms of editing, you can take on the role of the final copy editor and type the pieces so that they are ready for publication. Some teachers are uneasy with this way of publishing because it feels like you're fixing up the students' mistakes "for free." Remember, if you choose to publish this way, you'll still ask students to do as much editing as possible before the pieces come to you. You can also put your mind at ease by realizing that this is a process *professional* writers go through. Behind every published writer is a talented, tireless, and tenacious copy editor.

    Those less-than-enthused writers in the classroom respond to this way of publishing because they aren't required to rewrite their piece over and over again until it's perfect. Bonus: The writing looks professional when it's published, which helps kids feel more excited about writing.

  - **Teach your community to look at *content*, not just conventions.** A kindergarten teacher I know decided to showcase her students' writing on a prominent display board near the lobby of the school. She knew that staff members, community members, parents, and school board members would be stopping by to admire the children's work.

She also knew that most readers have a tendency to notice any conventional mistakes right away. So she placed a three-by-five-inch index card next to each piece of writing. On the card, she began to teach her community what to look for. She jotted down something specific that the writer was doing and then went on to explain why this specific component was beneficial to the reader. For example, next to Jacob's drawing of a tree in his backyard (with some labels that Jacob had added to show the parts of the tree), she wrote, *Notice how Jacob added veins to the leaves on his tree—what details! Those details help his reader know even more about his writing.*

Next to other students' writing, she wrote things like this:

- *Notice how DeShawn is using spaces between his words. The spaces help his reader know where one word ends and another word begins!*

- *Notice how Abby is writing down the sounds she hears in the words she is writing. In kindergarten, we call this 'brave spelling'! This kind of spelling will help her learn to spell conventionally as she continues to write!*

- *Did you see how Ethan used an ellipsis here? This creates a bit of suspense for his reader!*

These cards helped the community recalibrate their eyes to see not what was missing in the piece, but what was *there*.

- **Allow kids to edit themselves—and then communicate!** After kids have finished a piece of writing that will be published, give them at least a seventy-two-hour break from the piece. Then show them how to reread their writing with the eye of a proofreader or copy editor. Reminder: Before you ask kids to do this, let them see *you* do this with *your* piece of writing. They need to see what this kind of rereading and editing looks like!

Once kids have done as much editing work as they can, you are ready to publish! In this situation, communication is paramount.

You'll want to clearly communicate to the reader that the kids themselves edited their pieces.

One third-grade teacher invited the class to compile their published short stories into an anthology that was placed in the school library and available for checkout. The teacher added a letter as the first page of the anthology. At the top of the letter in big, bold, all-cap letters, the teacher had written, WE ARE EMERGING EDITORS. The teacher went on to explain that the kids were learning to edit their own work. He listed the various conventions that students were currently working on and gave the reader a heads-up that they would likely see a few errors in spelling, capitalization, and punctuation because the kids were still developing as writers and editors.

This kind of clear communication helps readers (parents, community members, other students in the school) understand that writing is a complex process and that kids (especially nine-year-olds) are at varying levels of proficiency when it comes to editing their own work.

How Can We Maximize Our Conventions Instruction?

1. **Use real-world examples.**

   When most of us think of using mentor texts, we typically think of using them to highlight particular craft moves, like speaking directly to the reader or using descriptive language or crafting a lead that will draw the reader in. While all of that is true, you can also use mentor texts to teach conventions.

   By using the work of others to highlight the conventions of print, we shift the focus of conventions from a list of rules that must be followed (or else!) to what conventions were always meant to be: clues and cues to help the reader better understand the text. Every mark on the page is there for a reason. So why not use mentor texts to show kids how other writers utilize and manipulate various conventions to help the reader understand (and hopefully *enjoy*) the text?

Here are some things to consider when using mentor texts to highlight and teach conventions:

- **Return to an old favorite.** Is there a book that you and your students love to read? Revisit that text, only this time with an eye on conventions! Use a document camera to enlarge a section of the book so that all students can see, or photocopy a small section so that partners can look carefully at the conventions on the page.

- **Engage in a conventions scavenger hunt.** You can do this in a number of ways. For example, host a punctuation scavenger hunt. As partners examine the text, ask, *Who can find a period?* Kids can scan the text, finding all of the periods the author has used. Then, zoom in on one example of how the author used a period and ask, *Why did the author put a period there? Chat with your partner about your thinking.* If every mark is there for a reason, then why is this period there? You're not looking for the correct answer here. You're inviting kids to be *curious* and think about why an author would use this kind of punctuation. This can be extended to other forms of punctuation or other conventions. For example, *Who can find a quotation mark? Who can find a question mark? Who can find a comma?* Again, don't forget: the most important question in this experience is *Why? Why did the author put a comma here? Why did the author use quotation marks here?* When we look at what published writers do in terms of conventions, we see these conventions not as the bane of our existence but as another tool that writers can use to impact and affect the reader. You can use one single page of text to examine and think about a variety of conventions. This kind of experience helps writers who might seem reluctant have a little *fun* with conventions rather than be weighed down by them.

- **Use an anchor chart to keep track of conventions that mentor writers use.** Keep a running anchor chart up (where all kids can see it) to keep track of the conventions you notice in mentor texts. When kids try a convention in their own writing, they can add their name to the section "Who else tried it?" An anchor

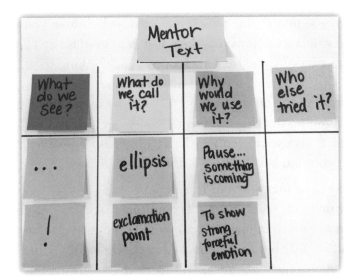

Use an anchor chart to keep track of the conventions that you find in mentor texts.

chart like this helps kids keep track of the variety of conventions that authors use and *why* they might use them.

- **Give kids time to read.** The more you see a convention of language used correctly when you read, the more you'll notice when something doesn't look (or sound) quite right in your own writing. So give kids plenty of time to read books that they can read and want to read. Wide reading leads to better writing.

2. **Think aloud as you write.**

It's not enough to simply show kids how proficient writers use conventions in a published and polished text. The real power comes when we crack open our thinking and let kids see *us* use conventions as *we* write. When we make our thinking about conventions visible, the mystery (and some of the panic) dissipates. Writers see that conventions are just another component that writers think about when they write.

When modeling your own thinking and writing, it's helpful to keep these things in mind:

- **Let yourself model the conventions you need in the piece you're writing.** It might seem logical to focus only on a particular convention when modeling, but that's not the way writers write.

When you model, don't be afraid to show kids how you use a variety of conventions. Let them watch as you use an ellipsis to create a bit of suspense. Crack open your thinking so kids can see *why* you are adding a capital there or a quotation mark here or a comma there. You're not expecting kids to immediately go off to write and master these conventions. Rather, you're showing them how writers use conventions based on what they are writing and what your students can reach for in their own writing.

- **Keep a tight focus in your instruction.** One of the mistakes I made early on in my own journey as a writing teacher was trying to teach too much in one lesson. I would set out to teach my kids about periods but get sidetracked in the midst of my instruction and remind them about capitals, correct spelling, and quotation marks. A mentor helped me rethink this practice by encouraging me to narrow my focus to one teaching point at a time. She said that when we focus our teaching, the learning can go much deeper. So, even though you model using a variety of conventions, focus your explicit teaching on just one. Zooming in on just one convention at a time helps writers who are hesitant feel empowered rather than overwhelmed by the world of conventions.

- **Show kids how you use tools to help you.** Not sure where that punctuation goes when you are adding dialogue? Let kids see you use a tool to help you! Perhaps you can return to a mentor text that you and your kids used when learning about quotations. Can't remember how to spell a word as you write in front of kids? Show them how you use a word wall, personal dictionary, classroom dictionary, print displayed in the classroom, or a friend to help you. Some writers in your classroom have the mistaken belief that when you grow up, you know all things. You are dispelling this myth and helping your students see that no writer knows *every rule* for *every convention.*

- **Model risk-taking.** If you play it safe in your own writing in front of kids, then they'll follow suit. So stretch yourself when it comes to conventions! Use a variety of punctuation or try a new kind of punctuation. Let kids see you spell a word that is just beyond your reach. When you show kids that it's OK to try something new (even if it bombs), you're sending the message that, in this classroom, you are focused on learning rather than perfection. This helps kids relax and be more willing to get something down on the page.

- **As you wrap up your thinking, invite students to try the new skill in their own writing.** If you show students how you use quotation marks in your piece, make it explicit that you're now asking *them* to try using quotation marks in *their* writing. It might sound like this: *Today I showed you how I use quotations when I add dialogue to my narrative. The quotation marks help my reader know who is speaking and what that person is saying. Today, as you continue working on your own narratives, try adding some quotation marks to help your reader. As you try to write, I'll come by and admire you.*

3. Coach individual writers.

It's important that you maintain a healthy perspective on conventions when you're working with students one-on-one as well. The truth is, what we focus on in these conversations will tell kids what we think is most important. If most of our conferences and conversations focus on capitalization, punctuation, spelling, and grammar, the message kids hear is that these components of writing are *the most important* components of writing. And if we focus on the minutiae of writing, this doesn't motivate those kids who are already less than enthused about writing. So, the question becomes, "How can our conversations with individual kids help them learn about conventions in a low-key and positive way?"

Here are some tips for maintaining a healthy perspective on conventions as you coach:

- **For the first reading, don't look at the writing.** Instead, ask the student to read the writing to you. (If the piece is long, ask the student to read a small section to you.) Most of us teachers have

red-pen eyes. We can look at a piece of writing and immediately see all of the mistakes in conventions. If we *listen* to the piece, rather than look at the piece, we might find it easier to focus on *content* and *craft*, instead of diving in to fix the conventions. Writers who might be hesitant, in particular, appreciate this approach because many of them already feel insecure when it comes to conventions.

- **Talk about conventions, just not all the time.** The key here, especially for less-than-enthusiastic writers, is not to focus *every* conversation on capitalization, punctuation, spelling, or grammar. Mix it up a bit! Most teachers find it helpful to jot down what they talk about each time they work with a particular student. That way, when you come to sit next to Johnny, you can look back and see what you talked about the last time you worked with Johnny. If you notice that you focused on ending punctuation, you can check in with a question like, *Last time* *you and I talked about adding punctuation to your sentences to help the reader better understand your writing. How's that been going for you?* Then you can pivot the conversation for today to a focus on a *different* component of writing, like using descriptive words to help the reader get a clear picture in their mind, or using a mentor text to craft an inviting hook or lead.

- **Use the phrase "as a reader."** I've mentioned this in other chapters, but it's worth repeating here. If you choose to focus your coaching on conventions, make sure the student understands *why* the convention matters to an actual reader. When you use the phrase "as a reader," kids see that they need to attend to conventions not because their teacher told them to, but rather because the conventions matter for a reader. And writing for an actual reader is a lot more motivating than writing for a teacher.

Here is what this might sound like:

- *As a reader, I had a hard time knowing that that was the word* broccoli. *What resources can you use to help you spell that word so that your reader knows that your mom had served your least favorite vegetable and that was broccoli?*

- *As a reader, I'm feeling a bit of suspense here. That's because you've added an ellipsis. When you do that, your reader knows something is coming and it adds a bit of interest for your reader.*

- *As a reader, I'm a bit confused. At the beginning of the piece, you're talking about events that happened a while ago, in the past. So you're using words like* hiked, talked, *and* looked. *These are what we call the past tense of verbs. Then, down here, you switch. You say, "We* see *a waterfall; we* drink *from our canteens." As a reader, I'm confused. The action words, or verbs, are telling me that this is happening right now. What can you do to help your reader know that all of this happened in the past?*

- **Use mentor texts.** If you've used a mentor text during your lesson about a particular convention, bring that book with you as you talk to kids one-on-one. That way, you can show kids what published writers do with conventions. This can be motivating because kids see that real writers use these conventions; this isn't just something they need to do for this particular assignment.

- **Use a celebratory and positive tone, rather than a corrective tone.** Let's face it. No one likes to be corrected, especially when we've worked hard on something complex, like writing. So, if each time we work with a child, we simply correct his conventions, he's going to shut down pretty quickly. For example, when you come alongside a kindergarten or first-grade writer, you could say, *Wow! You wrote a whole sentence! Do you know what goes at the end of a whole sentence?* This gives off a completely different vibe than, *Oops. You forgot a period here. Make sure you have a period at the end of your sentences.*

- **Ask questions.** Sometimes teachers think that writing conferences should focus on teaching something specific. While this is true, conferences also give us a chance to assess what kinds of understanding students are bringing to the conventions they are using. So, ask why!

  - *I see you added some quotation marks here. Tell me why you did that.*

  - *I notice that you used a capital letter here. Why did you do that?*

  - *I see that you've used a question mark here. Tell me why you chose to use a question mark here.*

  - *Wow! What a big word you used here! What resources did you use to spell that?*

When you work one-on-one with kids, you have a rare opportunity to shape kids' perceptions of conventions and help them engage with writing at the same time!

Closing Thoughts

Regie Routman (2005) said that students won't pay attention to conventions if they don't care about the writing. If we *overemphasize* conventions, some of our students will bow to the demands of perfection but produce writing that isn't actually worth reading. Conventions and content were always supposed to be married and live happily ever after. If our students are invested in their writing—if they write for audiences that matter to them about topics that matter to them—they will pay attention to conventions and ultimately become proficient writers who also *enjoy* writing.

Jackson, a kindergarten writer from Lincoln Elementary, can show us what this looks like in action. Jackson's teachers, Aly Weigel and Julie Frank, began a unit of study on persuasive writing. They taught their forty-three kindergartners (yes, forty-three!) that there is power in writing. Just as a magician uses a wand to make things happen, writers use words to make things happen. Aly and Julie showed students how they could use writing to solve problems and make their classroom and school even better. They also taught their students how to make their writing *readable*. Throughout the persuasive writing unit, Julie and Aly taught students how to use resources to spell words, how to leave spaces between their words, how to use various kinds of punctuation, and how to write the words legibly so that others could read and understand their important messages.

As the unit began, Jackson quickly identified a problem that he wanted to solve. His class did not have show-and-tell. He decided to use his "wand of words" to write his teachers a letter. Jackson knew his letter was going to important people in his life and he cared deeply about his topic, so he took care in the conventions he used.

His teachers responded to his letter and told him that they had thought about show-and-tell many times, but there were two main

Dear Mrs. Frank and Mrs. Weigel,

Can we please have show-and-tell? I think it would be fun. I like to bring toys to share with my friends. Will you let us?

Love, Jackson

problems: (1) there wasn't enough time for forty-three students to share and (2) bringing toys to school could be problematic because toys might get broken, lost, or stolen.

This did not stop Jackson.

He created a petition to show his teachers that he was not the only student in the classroom who was interested in having show-and-tell. Twenty-nine of his classmates signed the petition. Because he was so invested in the topic and the work he was doing, Jackson thought carefully about making his petition convincing *and* polished.

Jackson's teachers acknowledged that he had a strong case and that obviously the class was very interested in show-and-tell. Besides, what teacher could argue with the opportunity to practice the skill of communication? However, there were still some problems to work through. The teachers said that they were willing to meet with Jackson to discuss the details and come up with possible solutions.

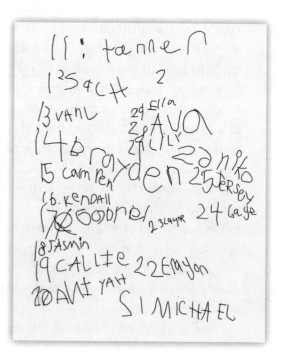

Do You Want Show-and-Tell?
To my kindergarten class: We can take turns. We can practice talking to the audience.

(In Jackson's petition, he has included signatures of twenty-nine classmates.)

Jackson agreed to the meeting and scheduled a time to meet before school. In preparation for his meeting, Jackson met with his sister's second-grade teacher, who did show-and-tell in her class, to ask her how it worked. He then crafted a final letter to bring to his meeting. Jackson wrote this letter twice because he felt that the first letter was difficult to read. This topic was important to Jackson, so the conventions (and neatness) mattered.

Jackson came to the meeting dressed for success in a suit and tie (just like he had seen his dad wear when he went to meetings). He came armed with his solutions letter and a cup of piping-hot coffee for each of his teachers. Together, Jackson and his teachers discussed his letter, and all agreed to give show-and-tell a try in the classroom.

When kids create pieces of writing that say something important, when they write about topics that are important to them, and when they know that the writing will be read by someone who matters, they take conventions seriously. They come to understand that conventions are there to support the message—to make the message readable. They also understand that conventions are not the be-all and end-all of writing. They develop and maintain a healthy perspective on conventions, which just might help them enjoy writing.

Following is a list of questions to consider as you take a reflective and honest look at your current practices in the hope of engaging all of the writers in your classroom.

If you're reading this book with a group of colleagues, use these questions to guide your shared conversation and learning.

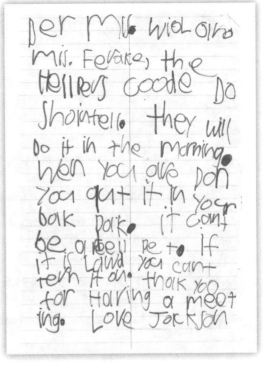

Dear Mrs. Weigel and Mrs. Frank,

The helpers could do show-and-tell. They will do it in the morning. When you are done, you put it in your backpack. It can't be a real pet. If it is loud, you can't turn it on. Thank you for having a meeting.

Love, Jackson

Questions for Reflection

1. What conventions am I currently focusing on in my classroom? What are the specific language standards in my state for my grade?

2. Do I notice kids tensing up when they write, anxious that everything needs to be perfect on the page? What can I do to help kids develop a healthy perspective on conventions?

3. Am I narrowing the focus of my teaching on one convention at a time when I teach? Or am I trying to teach too many conventions in each lesson?

4. What are some ways that I could publish student writing in my classroom? How might writing for an authentic reader change my students' perspective on conventions?

Chapter Seven

Shape Writing Identity Through Assessment

Good assessment should be a companion to learning, not a threat, but a help—to the teacher and to the student.

—Vicki Spandel, *Creating Young Writers*

A few years back, my husband and I attended an all-day parenting seminar. We spent a sunny Saturday inside a local community center sipping just-OK coffee and listening to several different speakers talk about a multitude of topics. Most of the speakers and topics we heard that day have faded from my mind. However, I remember with vivid clarity what I heard right before lunch from the licensed counselor, Doug Samsel. He started off by telling us that we, as parents, have the immense privilege and responsibility to co-author the identity and "life story" of our children.

Talk about pressure!

I swallowed hard and poised my pen to take down some notes.

One thing he said struck such a deep chord with me that I wrote it down word for word: "One of our jobs as parents is to discover our child's uniqueness, beauty, and complexity, and then read their identity back to them. We provide a variety of experiences for our children and then watch with marveled curiosity. This role as parents and co-authors of identity requires us to have the curiosity of Sherlock Holmes and the playful delight of Willy Wonka."

While he used these words to describe the unique (and, OK, kind of *daunting*) role of parents, I couldn't help but think that he had just uttered a perfect description of assessment.

As writing teachers, we provide a variety of writing experiences for our students where they can interact with words and sentences, paragraphs and pictures. When we assess students, we notice how they interact with these experiences. Part of our role as writing teachers is to approach our students' writing with *marveled curiosity*, noticing the uniqueness, beauty, and complexity that is found there. And then we have the privilege and awesome responsibility to read their unique, beautiful, and complex identity back to them.

Whoa.

With this in mind, assessment can feel significant (and more than a little bit daunting).

The truth is, we don't always think of assessment in the way that Doug Samsel described. Some of us might think writing assessment looks like this:

1. Assign a piece of writing.
2. Tell kids what is expected.
3. Collect the piece.
4. Assess it. Correct it. See if they did what they were supposed to do. Evaluate the writing. Decide if it's any good or not.
5. Give the student a grade.
6. Pass the writing piece back to the student.

But could this way of assessing student writers actually be *causing* students to avoid or dislike writing? Might it actually cause students to develop a negative identity about themselves as writers? Could it be that some of the students in our classroom who often try to avoid writing have been accidentally damaged by the assessment practices that they've endured? Writing is the author's heart on the page. When we respond to a child's writing, we are responding to the child's heart. It stands to reason that the way in which we respond to that writing requires some thought and consideration.

What if we took a step back and looked at writing assessment as an opportunity to approach a student (and their writing pieces) with a marveled curiosity? What if we saw assessment as an opportunity to discover a student's uniqueness, beauty, and complexity, and then used assessment to read that identity back to them? What if we viewed ourselves not as the corrector-in-chief but rather as a fun and quirky mix of Sherlock Holmes and Willy Wonka?

We have the immense privilege and awesome responsibility to coauthor the writing identity of our students. Let's tread lightly and carefully.

Reflect on Your Own Life as a Writer

Think back on your own life as a writer. Can you remember writing assessments that you endured as a student? Do you remember particular comments from teachers about your writing? Can you recall a particular grade that you received on a writing assignment? What kind of feedback did you receive through assessment? Has it shaped the way you approach writing?

Recently, I was talking about writing instruction, assessment, and feedback with a friend of mine. She confided that, when she was an elementary student, much of the assessment she received was in the form of red pen marks and comments strewn all over her work. "It was as if my teacher had performed an autopsy on my writing," she said. "There was nothing I could do to fix all of the things she had noticed; the paper was already turned in."

Can you relate to this experience? I know that I can.

While it's true that some of us were fortunate enough to have positive experiences with writing assessments and feedback, many of us carry with us less-than-positive memories.

John Kaag (2014), in an article written for *The New York Times*, put it this way: "Genuine criticism, the type that leaves an indelible mark on you as a writer, also leaves an existential imprint on you as a person (para. 4)."

It's true. The feedback we receive through assessment becomes a part of our writing identity. And we bring that identity with us into the classroom as teachers. Sadly, if we don't learn how to assess our students' writing in a way that nudges them to improve while keeping their dignity and confidence intact, we might end up repeating the kinds of negative assessment practices that we ourselves experienced as students.

What Does This Look Like in the Classroom?

How does this play out in the classroom? Am I suggesting that we all sit in a circle, hold hands, and repeat positive affirmations about our writing and ourselves as writers?

Not quite.

What I am suggesting is that we tread thoughtfully and carefully when we assess. I'm suggesting that we take a good, hard look at the assessment practices we are currently using and ask ourselves some tough questions to find out if these practices are helping or harming the writers in our classroom.

In the following sections, I've listed a few examples of what positive and productive assessment might look like in the classroom.

Kids and Teachers Talk About High-Quality Writing

If we're going to assess kids on whether or not they can create strong pieces of writing, it stands to reason that we should help them develop a sense of what strong pieces of writing look like and sound like. In Tamara Ward's fifth-grade classroom, students were creating public service announcements (PSAs). Before Tamara asked her students to delve into this writing project, she showed the students lots and lots of PSAs. Tamara asked her students to think about the question she had written at the top of a piece of chart paper: *What Makes a Good PSA?*

After watching several PSAs and talking about them with a partner, the students listed features of a strong PSA:

- *It includes strong visuals.*
- *The message is simple and clear.*
- *It has convincing language.*
- *It ends with a call to action.*

- *There's a clearly stated opinion.*

- *The opinion is supported by facts.*

- *It often gives the reader a website to visit for more information on the topic.*

This features chart was extremely helpful as students began writing their own PSAs. Tamara noticed that many of the students referred back to the chart to make sure they had included the features in *their* PSA. This list of features also helped students self-assess. They compared their PSA to the ones they had watched.

All writers in Tamara's room were engaged and inspired because they had seen what published PSAs looked like and sounded like. They knew what they were going for and *they* came up with the indicators of what a strong PSA was, instead of having the *teacher* decide what they needed to include.

Kids Take Ownership of Their Assessment

In some classrooms, teachers ask *the kids to self-assess* and set goals for themselves as writers. To do this, the teacher, together with the students, creates a list of possible goals.

Some of the goals reflect particular writing *skills*:

- *I'm working on capitalization.*

- *I'm working on making my writing legible for my reader.*

- *I'm working on spelling second-grade high-frequency words correctly.*

- *I'm working on making my writing easier for someone else to read.*

Some goals focus on a particular element of writing *behavior*:

- *I'm working on being brave with my spelling.*

- *I'm working on writing the whole time during the writing block.*

- *I'm working on finding a good spot where I can work.*

- *I'm working on writing a bit, stopping to reread, and then writing a bit more.*

Other goals highlight writing *craft*:

- *I'm working on using words that paint a picture in my reader's mind.*

- *I'm working on using precise words.*

- *I'm working on adding more describing words (adjectives) to my writing.*

- *I'm working on stopping to read my writing aloud to see if I need to change anything.*

Once the teachers and kids have recorded a list of writing goals, students look at their own writing and choose a goal that they would like to work on. Students write their name (or student number) on the chart next to the goal they have chosen. The teachers who have done this in the classroom tell me that the kids usually end up choosing goals that they (as teachers) would have chosen for them. They *know* what they need to work on!

The power in this kind of assessment comes when there's one more name (or number) on the chart: *yours!* Teachers can look through their own writing samples (while kids watch) and reflect on what they are doing well and what they want to work on. Once they've chosen a goal, teachers can talk about their goal whenever they are writing in front of kids. For example, a teacher might say, *You know that I am working on making my writing more legible for my reader, so as I work on my persuasive letter today, I'm going to keep that in mind. I'm going to slow down and really think about how I'm forming my letters.*

When students feel that they have reached their goal, they ask for a quick conference with the teacher. Together, the student and teacher look through the writing that the

Students placed a sticky note with their student number next to the goal they chose for themselves.

student has done. If both parties agree that the student has reached the goal, the student comes up to the chart and moves their name (or number) from their current goal to a new goal of their choosing.

This is empowering for all writers because they have *choice* of which goal to work on and they help decide when they have reached their goal. This also helps all writers know that they aren't alone. Some writers feel like they are the only ones who need to work on something. When they see that *everyone* has a goal, it helps dispel this myth.

Kids Know What They Are Doing Well and What They Are Working On

When my oldest son was in first grade, he wandered into my home office one afternoon while I was working. Noticing an outline that I had created for an upcoming session with teachers about reading comprehension, he exclaimed, "We've been learning about comprehension in my class, too! I'm really good at inferring when I read, and right now I'm working on synthesizing—you know, putting everything together when I read."

I looked at him, dumbfounded.

He was so matter-of-fact about his strengths and area of need. And he had the *language* to describe them. This didn't happen by accident. His teacher, Michele Beitel, talked openly with her students each day as she stopped by to chat with individuals about what they were doing as readers. This language that Michele (and her students) were using to talk about themselves as readers was as natural as talking about what the cafeteria was serving for lunch that day.

Some teachers find it helpful to keep a conferring record sheet in each child's writing folder. When a teacher stops by to confer with a student, they pull out the sheet of paper, jot down the date, and then write something that they notice the student doing really well in their writing. If the teacher has taught something specific during the conversation, they might also jot that down. This conferring record sheet lives in each kid's writing folder so they know exactly what they're doing well and what they're working on as a writer. Bonus: On a different day when the teacher comes back to chat with the same student, the teacher can look back on past notes to see what they and the child talked about last time, using that as a jumping-off point for their current conversation.

| Name _Hayden_____ |
| Writing |

Date	I am	I am working on
9/16	Telling my reader a lot of details!	Making my characters talk or move.
9/19	Making my characters talk in my narrative!	Adding movement (verbs)
9/23	Dialogue & movement are found in my narrative. My reader can picture it!	Being brave with my spelling.

The conferring record sheet helps the student know what they are doing well and what they are working on.

This kind of record keeping impacts writers in a positive way because writers know *exactly* what they're doing well *and* what they need to work on. They're goals are targeted, clear, focused, and attainable—all of the attributes that are helpful when setting goals!

Reality Check: *Standards and Rigor*

You might be thinking, "This all sounds fine. But in my district, kids are required to engage in on-demand writing assessments in which they write to a prompt. How does that work with what you're suggesting?"

Sometimes, well-meaning teachers believe that students will get better at on-demand, writing-to-a-prompt writing simply by writing to a different prompt each day. Sadly, this is not the case. More often than not, when we ask kids to write to a prompt each day, they don't become better writers. They simply learn to dislike writing.

The first challenge is the prompt. In the real world, we don't write to prompts. We write to people. We write to a specific person (or group of people) for a very specific reason. I would argue that if we don't know whom we are writing to and we don't value the purpose of the writing, we probably don't write at all. Also, a prompt often assumes a common experience that is often not shared. A couple of years ago, I spoke to a teacher who had given her kindergarten students the following prompt: *Teach someone how to make a pizza.* A few minutes after she sent the kids off to write, a student came up to her, looking bewildered. He looked up at her and said, *I've never made a pizza.*

Still, many of us work in districts where a write-to-the-prompt, on-demand writing assessment is part of our reality. So how can we live within this reality while still supporting and engaging all writers in our classroom? How can we help kids be successful with this kind of writing without creating even more kids who don't like to write?

My answer is simple: Teach this type of writing as a genre.

Let's imagine for a moment that we are teaching kids how to write a book review. We might follow these steps:

1. Immerse kids in the kind of writing they will be doing. Invite them to *read* lots of book reviews.

2. Create a chart that lists the features of this kind of writing. We might ask kids: *What makes a strong book review? What do these book reviews include?* Kids might notice that book reviews do things like

   - summarize the book without giving too much away

   - provide the reader with the title and author of the book they are reviewing

   - provide some reasons why you should (or shouldn't) read this book.

3. Model your own thinking as you begin crafting your own book review. The kids watch as you craft your own book review (using the features chart to help you). You might not write the *entire* book review, but you think aloud as you plan out what you'll say and maybe write a few sentences.

4. Invite kids to talk to a partner about their own book and plans for their own book review.

5. Send kids off to write, encouraging them to use the features chart to help them remember what to include in the book reviews.

6. Use the features chart to help you plan which minilessons to teach. For example, you might teach a lesson on how to clearly state your opinion about the book and then give some reasons to support that opinion.

On-demand writing assessment in which kids respond to a prompt is a particular kind of writing. It's a very specific *genre*. If we taught this kind of writing in much the same way we teach any other genre of writing, it might look like this:

1. Immerse students in the kind of writing they will be doing. Together, read lots of strong student samples from other on-demand writing assessments. These might be samples you've collected from years past or they may be samples you've collected from other classrooms, schools, districts, or states. (The internet is your friend here.)

2. Make a features chart about what makes a strong piece of on-demand writing. Kids might notice that this type of writing is, for example:

   - on topic
   - fully responsive to the prompt
   - legible
   - organized into sections or paragraphs
   - interesting.

3. Model your own thinking as *you* begin responding to a prompt. Engage in a think-aloud so that kids can see you think through (and maybe even struggle through) the prompt. Show students how you might plan out your writing for that particular prompt. I would argue that there are very few, if any, students who have ever watched as another writer read a prompt, analyzed it, and crafted a response.

4. Allow partners to talk. Give kids a different prompt from the one you used for your modeling. Give them time to chat with a partner. *How might you respond to this prompt? What are you thinking in terms of your response and your writing?*

5. Send them off to write, encouraging them to use the features chart to help them as they write.

6. Use the features chart to help guide your minilessons.

A unit on writing in response to a prompt shouldn't take an entire trimester. In fact, a couple of weeks would suffice.

If we look at on-demand writing to a prompt as just another writing genre, it helps take the fear and anxiety out of the equation. It takes the mystery out of it as well! It also helps students (and teachers) understand this is *one kind of writing* they'll do throughout their school career—not the *only* kind of writing that they'll do or the only kind of writing that matters. And, after engaging in this genre study, they'll have the tools they need to be successful anytime they engage in this kind of writing assessment.

How Can We Help Kids Develop a Positive Writing Identity Through Assessment?

So, how can we shape students' writing identity through assessment? How can we find out who the writers are in our classroom and what they need from us? And how can we do that in a way that will engage the less-than-enthusiastic writers in our classroom?

Here are a few ways to reframe our view (and our students' views) of assessment. Each of these ideas might just help students approach writing assessment with confidence and maybe even a bit of *joy*! As you read them, reflect on your own classroom and think about how you might use them, along with some ideas of your own.

- **Keep it simple.** I've found that, when it comes to assessment, we can get really complicated really quickly. One thing to keep in mind when we are considering shaping our students' identity through assessment is to keep it simple. I think that assessment is one of those words that has been hijacked in our country. It's come to mean a lot of different things that tend to cause stress for kids (and teachers). Overwhelmed and stressed-out teachers often lead to overwhelmed and stressed-out writers who don't like to write.

- **So, to counterbalance this, focus on simplicity.** One idea is to narrow assessment down to two main questions:

1. What is this writer doing well?
2. What might this writer need next?

Simplicity helps teachers (and writers who might appear to be reluctant) remain calm and peaceful rather than stressed and overwhelmed.

● **Assess *as you teach*.** It's a crisp fall morning in October and I've been invited to work with a class of kindergarten writers at Vargas Elementary in Sunnyvale, California. I'll be introducing an alphabet chart that kids can use to help them as they write. As the kids settle in on the floor in front of me, I pass out colorful and sturdy alphabet chart to each student. The chart shows each letter of the alphabet in order. Next to each letter, there's a picture and a word. (For example, next to the letter *U* there's a picture of an umbrella and the word *umbrella*.)

What do you notice? I ask as soon as I've passed out the last chart. *Talk to your partner about what you see and what you notice.*

Then I lean in and listen.

Look! There are pictures!

It's the whole alphabet! And the letters are in order!
[Singing] A B C D . . .

There are words. Look! Here's the word apple. *This one says* bear.

Here's a letter T! I have that letter in my name!

As I listen in to the chatter, I'm not simply marveling at how absolutely adorable they are (but just for the record, I am doing that). I'm also gathering invaluable assessment information.

Later that day, I work with a classroom full of fourth graders. I'm teaching them how to craft an introduction to their nonfiction pieces. I start off the lesson by saying, *Today, I'm going to show you something that writers do when they are writing nonfiction. But before I begin, I want to ask you a question: What is nonfiction? Share your thinking with your partner.*

As I listen in, I'm able to assess. What understandings are they bringing to this work? Where are the misconceptions? What is the teaching that has happened before I came?

The end of the day finds me with a class full of first graders who are learning to plan out their writing using multiple pages. After I choose a topic, I ask them to do the same. After I plan across my pages, I ask them to try it. Each time I ask kids to share their thinking with a partner, I listen. And I learn.

I learn that one child knows a lot about ice cubes (yep, ice cubes) and is planning to write all about this topic. I notice that many of the kids are going to write about taking care of a brother or sister. As I watch and listen to the kids plan across pages, I discover that some have a lot to say and write and some are still thinking.

This is all valuable assessment information that will be help me be a better writing teacher because I'll be able to tap into their personal interests, their background knowledge, their misconceptions, and their understanding. But it also helps me get to know them as humans, which ultimately is going to be the most powerful tool I have as a teacher. The connection that I have with them will help me enter their world and then invite them into mine.

This kind of ongoing, informal assessment helps students because it's nonthreatening and low-risk. Kids don't even realize that I'm assessing at all; they are simply engaged in thinking and talking.

● **Assess attitudes.** Yes, skills are important, but it's also important to check in and see how kids are *feeling* about writing and themselves as writers. You can do this through conversations that you have with kids, or if you want to be a little more formal about it, you can ask kids to periodically complete an attitude survey, like those shown in Figures 7.1 and 7.2 (available as reproducible online resources). The information you collect through these conversations or inventories will help you check in with kids and can lead to further conversations with individual students who might be feeling less than enthusiastic about writing.

If you ask these students to tell you more about their feelings about and experiences with writing, you'll have valuable information that could help you make changes so that the writing experiences they engage with in the classroom can be more positive and lead to more positive attitudes about writing and themselves as writers.

Figure 7.1

Name _____

Writing Attitude Survey

Read each statement and circle a number between 1 and 5.

A 1 means you *strongly disagree*; a 5 means you *strongly agree*.

I like writing at school.	1 2 3 4 5
I like writing at home.	1 2 3 4 5
I'm a good writer.	1 2 3 4 5
I can easily choose a topic.	1 2 3 4 5
Writing is fun.	1 2 3 4 5
Writing is important.	1 2 3 4 5
I get nervous when I write.	1 2 3 4 5
I look forward to writing time.	1 2 3 4 5

Figure 7.2

Name _____

Writing Attitude Survey

Read (or listen as your teacher reads) the following questions.

Circle the face that shows your feelings.

How do you feel when you write at school?

How do you feel when you write at home?

How do you feel when your teacher talks to you about your writing?

How do you feel when you see your friends write?

How would you feel if someone gave you writing supplies for a gift?

How do you feel when someone asks you to show them your writing?

Tip: One way that you'll know *for sure* that kids are enjoying writing and see themselves as writers is if you notice them writing during free time or even outside of school. One teacher recently told me that a parent called her and told her that her son (who had disliked writing in years past) asked for a writer's notebook and pens for his birthday. That's a powerful change in attitude!

● **Look at student work to plan instruction.** Assessment is only useful if it guides instruction. Yes, there are times when we need to report to stakeholders how students are doing. And yes, we need to check in with students so that we can communicate to others using report cards and grade books. But the real reason we assess is so that we know what kids need from us and our teaching.

Here's one way you can do this:

- Collect one writing sample from each student.

- Look through the samples and place them into three piles:

  1. Really strong

  2. Getting there

  3. Needs support.

- Now, look through each pile and look for patterns. In the "really strong" pile, what do you notice? Generally speaking, what are these students doing well? Make a list. (This will be a list of minilessons that might benefit other students.)

- Do the same for the other two piles of writing samples—the "getting there" pile and the "needs support" pile. Again, look for patterns. What do these pieces have in common? Are they disorganized? Formulaic and uninteresting? Weak in conventions? Make a list of the patterns you see. (This list will become a list of possible minilessons to teach.)

My rule of thumb is that if 40–50 percent of my students need a particular skill, I teach that skill in a whole-group lesson. On the other hand, if just a few students need a particular skill, I address it in one-on-one conferences.

This kind of assessment benefits all writers because kids don't feel singled out (and stressed out). You're looking at everyone's pieces to identify patterns of need. Also, there's no dreaded red pen involved at all!

- **Approach with curiosity rather than an eye for correcting.** Oftentimes we think of assessment as evaluative. We are trying to determine whether kids have mastered what we have taught. While that's true, assessment is also a means by which we learn about kids in general.

    One of the ways you can help shape students' writing identity (especially for those who appear to be reluctant) and give them a positive view of themselves as writers is to approach assessment with an air of curiosity instead of diving in to correct the mistakes. It's a mindset shift.

Instead of thinking, "All right. I'm going to check in on these writers and make sure they are following my directions," come with this mindset: "I'm going to check in with the writers in my classroom because I'm curious about what the kids are doing and thinking as writers."

This shift will help put students at ease because everyone tends to tense up a bit when they feel like someone is coming by to check on them and correct them. It's a very different feeling when you know that someone is coming to check in with you because they are curious about your work and your thinking.

How Can We Use Mentors, Modeling, and Coaching to Assess and Shape Writing Identity?

I hope you're starting to see assessment not as the big bad wolf coming to blow your peaceful classroom in but instead as a friendly neighbor who stops by to check in with you and see how things are going.

Once you've reframed assessment as a friend, you're ready to think about how to help less-than-thrilled writers tweak their own view of assessment.

Here are a few ideas:

1. **Use real-world examples.**

   It might seem strange to be thinking about mentor texts in a chapter on assessment, but if you think about it, mentor texts provide a perfect backdrop to assessment. I don't know about you, but I have never met a student who said, *You know, I really want to learn how to nail that W.4.4 standard.* But I have heard students say, *I want to write like Dav Pilkey,* or *I want to write like Nicola Davies.*

   Mentor texts provide that finished product that kids can aim for in their own writing; they are a much more approachable way for kids to think about writing and writing assessment; and they can serve as a measuring stick for other aspiring writers. When kids can see what other writers have done, they get a vision for what is possible in their own writing.

- **Use student work as mentors.** Save strong pieces of writing from year to year; these can become powerful mentor texts for kids. Recently, I was in a kindergarten classroom where the teacher was teaching her students how to craft persuasive letters. Before she wrote her own letter, she read a few that she had kept from previous years. She said, *This is Evelyn. She was a student in my class a couple of years ago. This is what she wrote.* I watched as these kindergarten writers leaned forward with eyes widened as the teacher shared these examples. It's one thing to see and hear a published piece of writing that is professionally bound and illustrated. It's quite another thing to hear a powerful and strong piece of writing that has been done by someone your own age!

- **After you read the text, ask kids to talk about it.** Whether you're using a published text or a student sample, ask kids to respond to the mentor texts they have heard. *What did you think? What did you like about this piece?* Zoom in not only on *what* the author said but *how* the author said it.

- **Use a rubric to assess the text.** This helps kids see that the rubric is not simply a list of things that must be done in their writing to get a good grade. They start to see that the features listed on the rubric are simply features of strong writing that readers enjoy.

- **Show students how you consider the mentor texts when you are writing.** It might sound like this: *I noticed that in Xavier's letter, he didn't just say that Bruno's has the best pizza in town. He gave a few reasons why he thought Bruno's had the best pizza. I think I'll try what Xavier did in my own letter. I'll give a few reasons for my opinion, too.* Or you could say, *One of the things I noticed that Madison added to her narrative was a lot of talking, or dialogue. This dialogue helped me, as a reader, feel like I was right there. I think I'll try that in my own writing.*

2. Think aloud as you write.

It's one thing to see the finished pieces from skilled writers. It's another thing to see a writer (that's you!) think about assessment and high-quality writing while they are writing. When we, as writing teachers, make our own thinking about assessment visible, the mystery (and some of the fear) fades. Writers who might appear to be reluctant—and all writers—see that real assessment isn't so much about a number or a grade. Assessment is about process, growth, and striving to create a piece of writing that says something valuable to a reader.

When modeling your own thinking and writing, it's helpful to keep these things in mind:

- **You go first.** If you use a rubric to assess student writing, it's only fair that the students have a chance to use that rubric to assess *your* writing as well. When you finish a piece of writing, place it under a document camera, hand kids the rubric (a kid-friendly version works best), and ask them to score your writing.

  I find this works best when kids work in pairs to analyze your writing and talk about scores. Then, check in with kids and see how you did. Ask them to report out your scores (it's helpful if they can defend the score by using the specific language from the rubric).

  When I've done this, I have found that I score well on some areas of the rubric and I score poorly on others. It's not that I'm *trying* to score poorly; it's just what happens on writers' first drafts. When I don't score well on a particular portion of the writing rubric, I can show students how this leads me to *revise*. I show kids how I zoom in on that *one* component of good writing that is found on the rubric and revise with that singular focus.

  This powerful experience moves mountains when it comes to helping all writers reengage. Kids are so used to being evaluated but rarely have the chance to evaluate their *teacher's* writing. This brings everyone's anxiety down a few notches because when you are vulnerable enough to put your writing out there to be scrutinized and evaluated, kids are more willing to do the same. And they'll likely see that, even though you are an adult, your writing still needs editing, revision, and *support*! When I've done this with kids, I've also noticed that kids have started to internalize the indicators on the rubric. They've begun to see the rubric as a *tool* to help them self-assess and revise rather than just the thing their teacher uses to give them a grade on their writing once they turn it in.

- **If you use a writing rubric, show students how it helps you *as you write*.** Show kids how you place the writing rubric next to you *as you write* and think about the indicators that are found on the rubric. If the rubric is well written, it will list components that good pieces of writing have. The rubric then becomes a tool to help you make your writing better—not just a checklist to complete so you can get a good grade.

  For example, if the rubric says something like "sequences more than two events in a narrative," you can think aloud as you write and reflect on your own writing. It might sound like this: *Hmm . . . I've told my reader about one event, but my reader might want to know what happens next. I've written about my dog running off, but I should probably let my reader know what we did next. Watch me as I add that to my piece. I think it will make my piece even stronger for my reader.*

- **Model thinking about *the reader*, not the grade.** When you think aloud and write in front of your students, avoid saying things like, *I want to get a 4 on this piece, so I should do this!* Instead, make it clear to kids that the reason you're aiming for the indicators on the rubric is not for the score but so that you can include important features of good writing that will help your reader understand and enjoy what they're reading.

3. **Coach individual writers.**

   Coaching and conferring are at the very heart of the writing classroom. When you coach and confer, you check in with individual students and gather information to help you tailor your instruction to meet individual needs. In other words, you *assess*!

During this one-on-one time, kids can tell you about their writing and themselves as writers. It's my opinion that there's no greater impact when it comes to writing identity than how these conversations go.

Here are a few things to keep in mind when you are coaching (and assessing) individual writers:

- **Ask questions.** If you're going to find out more about the writer (and their writing), it stands to reason that you'll want to ask some questions to get the conversation going. The questions can be general, like these:

  - *What are you most proud of so far in your writing?*
  - *Where are you feeling stuck?*
  - *Is there anything you want me to read for or listen for?*
  - *Is there any specific help you need from me?*

  You can also ask specific questions, like these:

  - *Tell me about your picture. What's going on in your picture?*
  - *Tell me about these quotation marks. Why did you decide to add them here?*
  - *You obviously know a lot about this topic! How did you become such an expert?*

- **Listen.** Listen more than you talk. In other words, you are going to need to be quiet long enough for the student to tell you what they are thinking! Let the kid talk, and then *really* listen. You can use what you hear to help you think about what this writer is doing well and what they might need next.

- **Start with celebration.** One of the most powerful things we can do when we coach an individual writer is to help them identify those things they are doing really well as writers. I've heard it said that we learn primarily by building on our strengths. It's important for kids to know what they are doing well so that they can keep doing it!

- **Use the phrase "as a reader."** I've mentioned this phrase in other chapters and I'll mention it here again. This simple, yet powerful, phrase helps teachers let go of their "teacher-ness"—if only for a moment—and instead approach a piece of writing simply as a reader.

  Saying, *As a reader, I had a hard time knowing where one word ends and another begins. What can you do to help your reader?* has a very different effect on a writer than saying, *You need to put spaces between your words.* Both interactions are assessment. Both interactions are building a student's identity as a writer. But the interaction that begins with "as a reader" preserves the dignity of the writer and puts the thinking back on the kid. On the other hand, when a teacher says, *You need to put spaces between your words,* the message sounds more like, *You didn't do it correctly.* One is an invitation to think about the reader, and one is a request for compliance.

- **Take notes on your conversations with students—and then show them what you wrote.** As I've mentioned earlier, some teachers find it helpful to jot down a few notes after they confer with a student; these notes become part of the big picture when it comes to assessment. If you do take notes during conferences, be mindful of what effect your note-taking might have on your students: it's unnerving to sit beside someone while they're scribbling things down about you. If you take notes during conversations, consider letting kids read your notes about the conference. This will help kids know what you find important in conferences and has the added benefit of giving you extra practice in framing your work as being curious and enthusiastic rather than judgmental.

- **Keep your red pen in your drawer.** I've never met *one* person who appreciates red (or any other color) ink all over their work, no matter how helpful the comments are. Marking on kids' work is *not* assessment and is *not* helpful. On the other hand, talking to kids about their writing *as they are writing*—providing clear, positive, and helpful feedback while they still have time to implement it—can be helpful.

Closing Thoughts

Your gaze is a mirror.

I recently heard an interview with writer and poet Jacqueline Woodson. During the interview, Woodson talked about how she read as a child (and how she still reads as an adult).

> I read slowly with my finger following beneath the words. I read the same passages over and over again and really just *inhaled* narrative in this way that it was part of all my senses. And I never saw it as a struggle. It was how I read. . . . But, you know, when you're a child and someone is saying this isn't how one should do this, you begin to question because it's adults and it's . . . it's their gaze that's the mirror for you at that age. (Zomorodi 2019)

I was driving and when I heard Jacqueline say this. I pulled over and stopped, her words still ringing in my ears. "It's adults and it's their gaze that's the mirror for you at that age."

There it is: *assessment*.

Our gaze—the way in which we look at our students and their writing—is a mirror for them. They look in that mirror and see someone who enjoys writing and one who does writing well, or they see someone who struggles. They see writing as something that they enjoy and something that is valuable, or they see writing as a skill that must be mastered at any cost.

Our gaze is the mirror.

I've listed some questions to consider as you take a reflective and honest look at your current practices in the hope of engaging all of your student writers.

If you're reading this book with a group of colleagues, use these questions to guide your shared conversation and learning.

Questions for Reflection

1. How am I assessing my students' writing? How are these assessments shaping my students' views of themselves as writers? How are they shaping their attitudes toward writing?

2. If my gaze is a mirror for my students at this age, what is my gaze showing them?

3. How can I provide feedback that is both helpful and respectful?

4. What baggage am I carrying with me in terms of writing? How was my writing evaluated when I was a student? What is my identity as a writer?

Chapter Eight

It Starts with Us

Finally, don't forget to breathe.

—Regie Routman, *Writing Essentials*

This book has focused almost completely on *students* who might appear reluctant or disengaged when it comes to writing. I've shared lots of different strategies meant to reignite the spark of energy and *joy* in our students.

Before we part ways, I'd like to leave you with a few things we can do as *teachers of writing* to reignite our *own* energy and joy.

So here a few tips to keep in mind as you journey on your way.

Live with Your Eyes Wide Open

Writers live with their eyes wide open. They think about their writing even when they aren't writing. They notice a leaf or the way the wind moves through the trees and they tuck these moments, images, and words inside a notebook or in the recesses of their mind to pull from later when they are writing.

Just as we teach writers to think about their writing even when they're not writing, we as writing teachers can think about instruction even when we're not teaching. No, I'm not suggesting that we bury ourselves in our work and think about teaching every moment of every day. But I do think it's helpful to be on the lookout for things in your life that you can use in your teaching.

Here's an example: Recently, I was standing at the security line in an airport. I noticed a poster outlining the state's upcoming change to a new form of ID. I quickly fished my phone out from my purse and snapped a photo of the poster, thinking to myself, "This poster would make a great real-world example of how writers convey information in a simple and direct format."

Start Small

Perhaps you're feeling ready to try some of the strategies in this book. If so, yay! Can I encourage you to start small? Instead of trying all of them or changing everything you are doing in the classroom at once, pick one chapter to focus on. Or pick one strategy in one chapter to start with. If that small change or single strategy goes well, build on that success as you launch into the next one. Don't try to accomplish everything at once. Start small and let success build on success.

Be Thoughtful

The lessons we plan and the writing experiences we provide to students don't need to be flashy or fancy. It's more important that our lessons and writing experiences be meaningful, relevant, and purposeful.

I keep these questions at the forefront of my mind whenever I am planning a lesson or writing experience for kids:

- **Is it meaningful?** Is what I'm about to ask my students to do meaningful, or is it simply a writing *task*?

- **It is purposeful?** Is the writing I'm asking students to do serving a purpose other than simply checking a box to say that we did it? Is this writing going to impact an actual reader inside or outside the classroom?

- **Is this something that real writers do?** Do all writers fill out a graphic organizer each time they write? Do real writers recopy everything they write until it is correct? Do published writers write in five-paragraph form? If it's not something that *actual* writers do, then it's probably not meaningful or purposeful either.

- **Would I be engaged in this work?** Is this an experience that I would enjoy doing? If not, chances are that students won't enjoy it either.

Focus on Relationships

In her book *More Than Meets the Eye*, Donna Skolnick says, "Most children who step down from the big yellow bus in the morning want to be greeted in their classroom by someone they care about and like and someone who cares about and enjoys being with them" (2000, 14). As a mom, I've noticed that my children take more risks, make more growth, and enjoy learning when they have a good relationship with the teacher. Yes, it's important that you know the *content*, but it also helps when kids feel that you know *them*, understand that you value them, and see you working to build solid relationships with them. Key to teaching is building relationships.

Live a Joyfully Literate Life

There's not one shred of evidence that shows a positive correlation between the hours that you (as a teacher) spend at school and student success. There's no prize for who works the most hours. In fact, I would argue that you just might be a more effective, energized, and interesting teacher if you strive to live a joyfully literate life outside of school.

So, read professionally. Read for pleasure. Get lost in an audiobook while you take a walk or listen to a podcast as you commute. Sign up for a class and learn something new. Experience what it's like to be lost in a book, deeply engaged in a topic, or on the learning side of a classroom. Not only do these experiences make us more interesting and joyful humans, but they also let us bring these experiences into our teaching so that we stay fresh and invigorated.

✦Bonus: When you have interests to draw from beyond school, you always have something to write about when you are modeling your own writing in front of kids.✦

Be a Writer

My son is learning to play the trumpet. He recently came home with the sheet music for an upcoming concert. He was stuck on a particularly challenging section. Confession time: I had a really hard time helping him! Even with a master's degree in teaching and decades of teaching experience, I found myself ill-equipped to teach him or coach him in any meaningful way. Why? I don't play the trumpet.

It's really hard (in fact, I would say almost impossible) to teach someone to do something that you don't do yourself. What my son needed in that moment of struggle was someone who knew how to play the trumpet. *They* would be able to show him a fingering that worked for them or teach him how to adjust his embouchure.

If we are going to be teachers who help reignite the spark of writing in our students, we're going to need to make sure our own spark for writing is ignited. The more we write, the more we learn about writing. The more we learn about writing, the more we are able to teach and coach other writers.

Learn from Others

Along with being a writer, learning from others has had the greatest impact on my growth as a writing teacher (and, therefore, the greatest impact on the energy and engagement in my writing classroom).

The more I watch other teachers teach and invite them to watch me, the more I grow and learn and stretch myself as a person, a learner, and a teacher. Friends, teaching is not an individual sport. It's a team sport. We desperately need each other. So fling wide open the doors of your classroom and let others in! And then ask if others will do the same for you.

Keep Your Eye on the Prize

In her book *Bird by Bird*, Anne Lamott wrote:

> Writing has so much to give, so much to teach, so many surprises. That thing you had to force yourself to do—the actual act of writing—turns out to be the best part. It's like discovering that while you thought you needed the tea ceremony for the caffeine, what you really needed was the tea ceremony. The act of writing turns out to be its own reward. (1997, xxvi)

I recently heard an interview with the comedian Jenny Slate. She had just published a collection of personal essays called *Little Weirds*. As I listened, I was struck by what she said about her experience with writing.

> Writing this book . . . you know, first I kind of meant to write something else. And then I started to write things to soothe myself and I started to like to read my [writing] to myself. . . . I started to really find words that I loved and now they won't go away. (Cornish 2019)

As Lamott and Slate remind us, there's more to writing than simply putting pencil to paper and completing an assignment. The goal of all this planning and teaching and conferring and assessing is, simply, for kids to fall in love with writing. We want kids to find words that they love and never let them go. We want kids to see writing as a way to connect with others, share ideas, and engage in civil discourse. We want kids to know that writing is a powerful tool that they can use to think, reflect, remember, and influence others. We want kids to discover that the act of writing is its own reward. We want them to know, deep in their bones, that writing has so much to give and so much to teach.

We want kids to live joyfully literate lives.

It starts with us.

REFERENCES

Anderson, Carl. 2000. *How's It Going? A Practical Guide to Conferring with Student Writers.* Portsmouth, NH: Heinemann.

Anderson, Jeff. 2005. *Mechanically Inclined: Building Grammar, Usage, and Style into Writer's Workshop.* Portland, ME: Stenhouse.

_____. 2007. *Everyday Editing: Inviting Students to Develop Skill and Craft in Writer's Workshop.* Portland, ME: Stenhouse.

Applebee, Arthur N., Judith A. Langer, Martin Nystrand, and Adam Gamoran. 2003. "Discussion-Based Approaches to Developing Understanding: Classroom Instruction and Student Performance in Middle and High School English." *American Educational Research Journal* 40 (3): 685–730.

Atwell, Nancie. 1998. *In the Middle: New Understandings About Writing, Reading, and Learning.* 2nd ed. Portsmouth, NH: Heinemann.

Ball, Arnetha, and Marcia Farr. 2003. "Language Varieties, Culture, and Teaching the English Language Arts." In *Handbook of Research on Teaching English Language Arts*, edited by James Flood, Diane Lapp, James R. Squire, and Julie M. Jensen, 435–45. 2nd ed. Mahwah, NJ: Erlbaum.

Barshay, Jill. 2019. "Scientific Evidence on How to Teach Writing Is Slim." *The Hechinger Report*, November 4. https://hechingerreport.org/scientific-evidence-on-how-to-teach-writing-is-slim/.

Boswell, Kelly. 2016. *Write This Way: How Modeling Transforms the Writing Classroom.* North Mankato, MN: Maupin House.

_____. 2017. *Write This Way from the Start: The First 15 Days of Writer's Workshop.* North Mankato, MN: Maupin House.

Calkins, Lucy. 1986. *The Art of Teaching Writing.* Portsmouth, NH: Heinemann.

_____. 2003. *The Nuts and Bolts of Teaching Writing.* Portsmouth, NH: FirstHand.

_____. 2003. *Units of Study for Primary Writing: A Yearlong Curriculum.* Portsmouth, NH: FirstHand.

Collins, Allan, John Seely Brown, and Susan Newman. 1986. *Cognitive Apprenticeship: Teaching the Craft of Reading, Writing and Mathematics.* BBN-6459. Cambridge, MA: Bolt Beranek and Newman.

Cornish, Audie. 2019. "'Sorrow Is Not the Same as Pessimism': Comedian Jenny Slate." *All Things Considered*, She's Funny series, November 18. NPR. www.npr.org/2019/11/18/779412430/sorrow-is-not-the-same-as-pessimism-comedian-jenny-slate.

Cremin, Teresa. 2006. "Creativity, Uncertainty and Discomfort: Teachers as Writers." *Cambridge Journal of Education* 36 (3): 415–33.

Culham, Ruth. 2003. *6 + 1 Traits of Writing: The Complete Guide, Grades 3 and Up*. New York: Scholastic Professional Books.

Daniels, Harvey, and Steven Zemelman. 1985. *A Writing Project: Training Teachers of Composition from Kindergarten to College*. Portsmouth, NH: Heinemann Educational Books.

Daniels, Harvey, Steven Zemelman, and Nancy Steineke. 2007. *Content-Area Writing: Every Teacher's Guide*. Portsmouth, NH: Heinemann.

Dorn, Linda J., and Carla Soffos. 2001. *Scaffolding Young Writers: A Writer's Workshop Approach*. Portland, ME: Stenhouse.

Duke, Nell K., and V. Susan Armistead. 2003. *Reading and Writing Informational Text in the Primary Grades*. New York: Scholastic Teaching Resources.

Elbow, Peter. 1998. *Writing Without Teachers*. New York: Oxford University Press.

———. 2004. "Write First: Putting Writing Before Reading Is an Effective Approach to Teaching and Learning." *Educational Leadership* 62 (2): 9–13.

Fisher, Bobbi. 1995. *Thinking and Learning Together: Curriculum and Community in a Primary Classroom*. Portsmouth, NH: Heinemann.

Fisher, Douglas, and Nancy Frey. 2003. "Writing Instruction for Struggling Adolescent Readers: A Gradual Release Model." *Journal of Adolescent and Adult Literacy* 46 (5): 396–407.

Fisher, Douglas, and Carol Rothenberg. 2008. *Content-Area Conversations: How to Plan Discussion-Based Lessons for Diverse Language Learners*. Alexandria, VA: Association for Supervision and Curriculum Development.

Fletcher, Ralph J. 1996. *A Writer's Notebook: Unlocking the Writer Within You*. New York: HarperTrophy.

_____. 2006. *Boy Writers: Reclaiming Their Voices*. Portland, ME: Stenhouse.

Fletcher, Ralph J., and JoAnn Portalupi. 2007. *Craft Lessons: Teaching Writing, K–8*. 2nd ed. Portland, ME: Stenhouse.

Fox, Mem. 1988. "Notes from the Battlefield: Towards a Theory of Why People Write." *Language Arts* 65 (2): 112–25.

Freeman, Yvonne S., and David E. Freeman. 2002. *Closing the Achievement Gap: How to Teach Limited-Format Schooling and Long-Term English Learners*. With Sandra Mercuri. Portsmouth, NH: Heinemann.

Gallagher, Kelly. 2011. *Write Like This: Teaching Real-World Writing Through Modeling and Mentor Texts*. Portland, ME: Stenhouse.

Graves, Donald H. 1983. *Writing: Teachers and Children at Work*. Exeter, NH: Heinemann Educational Books.

_____. 1985. "All Children Can Write." *Learning Disabilities Focus* 1 (1): 36–43.

_____. 1994. *A Fresh Look at Writing*. Portsmouth, NH: Heinemann.

_____. 1998. *How to Catch a Shark: And Other Stories About Teaching and Learning*. Portsmouth, NH: Heinemann.

Graves, Donald, and Virginia Stuart. 1985. *Write from the Start: Tapping Your Child's Natural Writing Ability*. New York: New American Library.

Harwayne, Shelley. 2001. *Writing Through Childhood: Rethinking Process and Product*. Portsmouth, NH: Heinemann.

Howard, Mary. 2012. *Good to Great Teaching: Focusing on the Literacy Work That Matters*. Portsmouth, NH: Heinemann.

Hoyt, Linda, and Kelly Boswell. 2012. *Crafting Nonfiction Intermediate: Lessons on Writing Process, Traits, and Craft*. Portsmouth, NH: Heinemann.

Hoyt, Linda, Jane Olson, Kelly Davis, and Kelly Boswell. 2011. *Solutions for Reading Comprehension: Strategic Interventions for Striving Learners, K–6*. Portsmouth, NH: Heinemann.

Hoyt, Linda, and Teresa Therriault. 2008. *Mastering the Mechanics, Grades 6–8: Ready-to-Use Lessons for Modeled, Guided, and Independent Editing*. New York: Scholastic.

Kaag, John. 2014. "The Perfect Essay." *The New York Times*, May 15. Opinion sec. http://opinionator.blogs.nytimes.com/2014/05/05/the -perfect-essay/?_php=true&_type=blogs&_php=true&_type=blogs& _php=true&_type=blogs&_r=2&.

Keene, Ellin Oliver, and Matt Glover. 2015. *The Teacher You Want to Be: Essays About Children, Learning, and Teaching*. Portsmouth, NH: Heinemann.

Kittle, Penny. 2008. *Write Beside Them: Risk, Voice, and Clarity in High School Writing*. Portsmouth, NH: Heinemann.

Krashen, Stephen. 2003. *Explorations in Language Acquisition and Use: The Taipei Lectures*. Portsmouth, NH: Heinemann.

Lamott, Anne. 1997. *Bird by Bird*. New York: Anchor Books.

Lane, Barry. 1999. *Reviser's Toolbox*. Shoreham, VT: Discover Writing.

Mason, Pamela A., and Emily Phillips Galloway. 2012. "What Children Living in Poverty *Do* Bring to School: Strong Oral Skills—Let Them Talk!" *Reading Today* 29 (4): 29–30.

Montana Office of Public Instruction. 2011. *Montana Content Standards for English Language Arts and Literacy—First Grade*. Helena: Montana Office of Public Instruction. https://opi.mt.gov.

Murray, Donald M. 1978. "Write Before Writing." *College Composition and Communication* 29 (4): 375–81.

———. 2009. *The Essential Don Murray: Lessons from America's Greatest Writing Teacher*. Edited by Thomas Newkirk and Lisa C. Miller. Portsmouth, NH: Boynton/Cook.

National Governors Association (NGA) Center for Best Practices and Council of Chief State School Officers (CCSSO). 2010. *Common Core State Standards*. Washington, DC: NGA Center for Best Practices and CCSSO. www.corestandards.org.

Newkirk, Thomas. 1988. *Understanding Writing: Ways of Observing, Learning, and Teaching*. 2nd ed. Portsmouth, NH: Heinemann.

———. 2002. *Misreading Masculinity: Boys, Literacy, and Popular Culture*. Portsmouth, NH: Heinemann.

Newkirk, Thomas, and Penny Kittle, eds. 2013. *Children Want to Write: Donald Graves and the Revolution in Children's Writing*. Portsmouth, NH: Heinemann.

Oczkus, Lori D. 2007. *Guided Writing: Practical Lessons, Powerful Results.* Portsmouth, NH: Heinemann.

O'Donnell-Allen, Cindy. 2012. "The Best Writing Teachers Are Writers Themselves." *The Atlantic*, September 26. www.theatlantic.com /national/archive/2012/09/the-best-writing-teachers-are-writers -themselves/262858/.

Ouellette, Gene, and Monique Sénéchal. 2017. "Invented Spelling in Kindergarten as a Predictor of Reading and Spelling in Grade 1: A New Pathway to Literacy, or Just the Same Road, Less Known?" *Developmental Psychology* 53 (1): 77–88.

Portalupi, JoAnn, and Ralph J. Fletcher. 2001. *Nonfiction Craft Lessons: Teaching Information Writing, K–8.* Portland, ME: Stenhouse.

Ray, Katie Wood. 1999. *Wondrous Words: Writers and Writing in the Elementary Classroom.* Urbana, IL: National Council of Teachers of English.

_____. 2002. *What You Know by Heart: How to Develop Curriculum for Your Writing Workshop.* Portsmouth, NH: Heinemann.

Ray, Katie Wood, and Lisa B. Cleaveland. 2004. *About the Authors: Writing Workshop with Our Youngest Writers.* Portsmouth, NH: Heinemann.

Ray, Katie Wood, and Matt Glover. 2008. *Already Ready: Nurturing Writers in Preschool and Kindergarten.* Portsmouth, NH: Heinemann.

Ray, Katie Wood, and Lester L. Laminack. 2001. *The Writing Workshop: Working Through the Hard Parts (and They're All Hard Parts).* Urbana, IL: National Council of Teachers of English.

Routman, Regie. 2000. *Conversations: Strategies for Teaching, Learning, and Evaluating.* Portsmouth, NH: Heinemann.

_____. 2005. *Writing Essentials: Raising Expectations and Results While Simplifying Teaching.* Portsmouth, NH: Heinemann.

Schumacher, John. 2019. "The Love of Books Tour." Presented at the North Dakota Literacy Association Summer Institute, June 3, Minot, North Dakota.

Skolnick, Donna. 2000. *More Than Meets the Eye: How Relationships Enhance Literacy Learning.* Portsmouth, NH: Heinemann.

Smith, Aaron, Skye Toor, and Patrick van Kessel. 2018. *Many Turn to YouTube for Children's Content, News, How-to Lessons.* Washington, DC: Pew Research Center.

Spandel, Vicki. 2004. *Creating Young Writers: Using the Six Traits to Enrich Writing Process in Primary Classrooms.* Upper Saddle River, NJ: Allyn and Bacon.

_____. 2005. *Creating Writers: Through 6-Trait Writing Assessment and Instruction.* 4th ed. Boston, MA: Allyn and Bacon.

Stead, Tony. 2002. *Is That a Fact? Teaching Nonfiction Writing, K–3.* Portland, ME: Stenhouse.

_____. 2006. *Reality Checks: Teaching Reading Comprehension with Nonfiction, K–5.* Portland, ME: Stenhouse.

Tobin, Lad. 1993. *Writing Relationships: What Really Happens in the Composition Class.* Portsmouth, NH: Boynton/Cook.

Zemelman, Steven, and Harvey Daniels. 1998. *Best Practice: New Standards for Teaching and Learning in America's Schools.* 2nd ed. Portsmouth, NH: Heinemann.

Zomorodi, Manoush. 2019. "Teaching for Better Humans." *TED Radio Hour* (podcast), September 20. NPR. https://one.npr.org/?sharedMediaId=761342972:762277284.

Zumbrunn, Sharon, and Keegan Krause. 2012. "Conversations with Leaders: Principles of Effective Writing Instruction." *The Reading Teacher* 65 (5): 346–53.